△.090.GREEK REVIVAL

STUDIES IN ARCHITECTURE

EDITED BY ANTHONY BLUNT AND RUDOLF WITTKOWER

VOLUME VIII

SOURCES OF GREEK REVIVAL ARCHITECTURE

DORA WIEBENSON

SOURCES OF
GREEK REVIVAL
ARCHITECTURE

DORA WIEBENSON

SCHOOL OF ARCHITECTURE, UNIVERSITY OF MARYLAND

1969

A. ZWEMMER LTD
LONDON

Contents

List of Plates

List of Abbreviations

AA. James Stuart and Nicholas Revett. *The Antiquities of Athens*. London, 1762–1830. 5v.

AB. Art Bulletin

AL. Année littéraire (ed. Fréron). Amsterdam. 1754–1790. 292v.

AR. Architectural Review

AReg. Annual Register. London. 1758–1862. 104v.

Balbec. Robert Wood and James Dawkins. *The Ruins of Balbec, otherwise Heliopolis in Coelosyria*, London, 1757

BM. The British Museum

BSBA. Bibliothèque des sciences et des beaux-arts. The Hague. 1754–1780. 50v.

BSW. Bibliothek der schönen Wissenschaften und der freyen Künste. Leipzig. 1757–1765. 12v.

CD. Correspondance des directeurs de l'Académie de France à Rome avec les surintendants des bâtiments. Paris, 1887–1908. 18v.

CR. Critical Review; or, Annals of Literature (ed. Smollett, etc.) London. 1756–1790. 70v.

DNB. Dictionary of National Biography

EM. European Magazine and London Review. London. 1782–1825. 87v.

ERO. Edinburgh Record Office

GGA. Göttingische gelehrte Anzeigen. (ed. Gesellschaft der Wissenschaften zu Göttingen). Göttingen. 1739+. (1753–1801, *Göttingische Anzeigen von gelehrten Sachen*)

GL. Gazette littéraire de l'Europe. Paris and Amsterdam. 1764–1784. 124v.

GM. Gentleman's Magazine. London. 1731–1907. 303v. (1736–1833, *Gentleman's Magazine and Historical Chronicle*)

JB. Journal brittanique. The Hague. 1750–1757. 24v.

JE. Journal encyclopédique ou universel. Liége, Bouillon and Brussels. 1756–1793

JRIBA. Journal of the Royal Institute of British Architects

JS. Journal des sçavans. Paris. 1665–1792

JSAH. Journal of the Society of Architectural Historians

JWCI. Journal of the Warburg and Courtauld Institutes

LG. London Gazette

LM. London Magazine; or Gentleman's Monthly Intelligencer. London. 1732–1783. 52v.

MF. Mercure de France. Paris. 1672–1820

MR. Monthly Review. London. 1749–1789. 81v.

NAE. Nova acta eruditorum. Leipzig. 1732–1776. 32v.

NAG. Neueste aus der anmüthigen Gelehrsamkeit. Leipzig. 1751–1762. 12v.

NBSW. Neue Bibliothek der schönen Wissenschaften und der freyen Künste. Leipzig. 1765–1806. 72v.

Palmyra. Robert Wood and James Dawkins. *The Ruins of Palmyra, otherwise Known as Tedmore, in the Desart.* London. 1753

PV. Procès-verbaux de l'Académie Royale d'Architecture (ed. H. Lemonnier). Paris. 1911–1929. 10v.

RIBA. The Royal Institute of British Architects

Ruines. Julien-David LeRoy. *Les ruines des plus beaux monuments de la Grèce . . .* Paris, 1758 (2nd ed. 1770)

Spalatro. Robert Adam. *Ruins of the Palace of the Emperor Diocletian at Spalatro in Dalmatia.* London. 1764

UM. Universal Magazine. London. 1747–1803. 113v.

Preface

THE archaeological publications that appeared during the last half of the eighteenth century have been recognized for some time to be influential in the formation of Neo-classical taste, and for this reason deserve more concentrated attention than they have been accorded to date. The present investigation of the history of these publications and of their interconnection with architectural theory and taste prior to the Greek Revival is intended to fill at least partially this gap in our knowledge.

The facilities and courteous assistance of the staffs of Avery Library at Columbia University, the New York Public Library, the British Museum, the Library of the Royal Institute of British Architects, and the National Monuments Record have been indispensable in the preparation of this work. It was made financially possible by grants from the American Association of University Women, the American Philosophical Society, and the Samuel H. Kress Foundation. The original idea was formulated in a doctoral dissertation for New York University. I am deeply indebted to Professor Rudolf Wittkower for his generous and invaluable editorial assistance. Mr John Harris read an early draft and has made helpful suggestions. The gracious permission of the Society of Dilettanti has made it possible for material from their Minutebooks and Letterbooks to be included. Miss Jean M. H. Mylne has kindly permitted me to read and quote from the Mylne correspondence. Translation of Latin passages was made with the assistance of Mrs Laszlo Baranszky-Job.

Introduction

THE area of the Levant is composed of the countries at the eastern
end of the Mediterranean. Before the region was of archaeological
significance the traveller went there for many other reasons: to
form part of a diplomatic mission, to gather scientific information, to
perform a religious pilgrimage, to engage in a business venture, or simply
for adventure. The traveller's observations were generally comprehensive
and encyclopaedic. He was concerned with modern, ancient, historical,
literary, geographical, botanical, and climatic characteristics of the area,
as well as the dress and customs of the people. Often his experiences and
the data he accumulated were published in journals or guide books, but
prior to the eighteenth-century archaeological publications contained
little visual material.

Indeed, within this wide framework, the ancient sites were of peri-
pheral interest; they generally were visited for their historical importance, recorded in literature, rather than for their architectural value. The
monuments of classical Greece especially were dissociated from the direct
observation of the travellers, for ancient Greek architecture played a role
in European tradition that had no immediate connection with the Levant.
According to this tradition, the ancient architecture of Greece not only
was the source of Western architecture, but also represented essential
beauty and perfection of form, expressed in these monuments through
proportional relationships. The secret of these proportional relationships
was, up to the mid-eighteenth century, considered to be lost.

Heightened interest in the Levant in the eighteenth century was due
partly to European desire for cultural reform through a return to the
origins of art: a major motivation for the archaeological expeditions was
the hope of rediscovering the lost ideal proportions of Greece through
accurate measurements of the antique monuments. At this time it also
became possible for private individuals to voyage to the Levant in com-
parative safety, due to the greater policing of the Mediterranean. Journey-

ing purely for their own edification, these travellers brought new dimensions of interpretation and a freshness of vision to the exploration of the ancient sites. Moreover, their method of investigation followed the pattern of empirical observation and recording of facts that had become a characteristic method for travellers to the Levant.

From the reports of the monuments brought back by the archaeological traveller, it became evident that there were two disparate concepts of ancient Greece. One was its unique physical presence, now realized in visual presentations based on direct observation; the other, its idealization, realized through traditional interpretations of classical literature. The various attempts to resolve the contradictions between the traditional attitudes and the original material were to create major developments in architectural theory and taste during the last half of the eighteenth century.

The form which these reports of the Levant took was generally that of the archaeological publication: the first to be conceived, and the most important of the group, as much from the interest that its conception aroused as from its later influence, was Stuart's and Revett's *Antiquities of Athens*. Of necessity this work occupies a major position in this study, and it is with this work that we begin.

CHAPTER I

External History of the
Antiquities of Athens

T HE first idea of a publication devoted to ancient Athenian monuments illustrated after drawings measured at the site is connected
with the name of Gavin Hamilton (1723–1798).[1] Indeed, Hamilton's speculative turn of mind qualified him as a medium for the predic-
tion of trends in taste. His early orientation toward the relation of classical antiquity to contemporaneous art, his publication of a Homeric series
of engravings at the opportune moment for maximum reception, and his
engagement in a lucrative sale of excavated antique sculptures,[2] made him
a potential source for the original conception of the *Antiquities of Athens*.

It is possible that Hamilton communicated his idea to Nicholas Revett
(1720–1804), or that the idea was formulated separately by each of these
men, in the spring of 1748 when they made a trip to Naples with James
Stuart and Matthew Brettingham. Revett, reporting in a letter on the
early stages of the project,[3] made an optimistic calculation of the profits
to be made from the publication. At this stage the plan, in which all the
work including the engraving of the plates was to be done by the authors
in the space of four years, was as impractical as it was enthusiastic. Indeed,
Revett does not seem to have been able to formulate the undertaking in

1. See Appendix I, entry B.

2. For Hamilton's business activities, see Adolf Michaelis, *Ancient Marbles in Great Britain*,
Cambridge, 1882, pp. 73–76; James Dallaway, *Anecdotes of the Arts in England*, London, 1800, pp.
364—381, "Extracts of Letters from Gavin Hamilton, at Rome, to Charles Townley, Esq. Relative
to his Discovery of Marbles in that Vicinity"; *A Catalogue of the Ancient Marbles at Lansdowne House,
Based on the Work of Adolf Michaelis*, ed. Arthur Hamilton Smith, London, 1889 (containing
Hamilton correspondence); and David Irwin, "Gavin Hamilton: Archaeologist, Painter, and
Dealer", *AB*, XLIV, June 1962, pp. 92–95.

3. See Appendix I, entry B.

B

practical terms, nor to have possessed the drive necessary to carry forth such an operation as the *Antiquities*. That we know little about him may be less the result of loss of information than of the fact that Revett, though gifted, was aware of his limitations, and was willing to play a minor and retiring role. His life up to 1748 was undistinguished.[4] The second son of an established family, he was brought up as a gentleman, sailed to Italy (probably on a purely educational tour) and entered the studio of Benefial on his arrival in Rome in 1742. Like Stuart, he was considered to be a painter rather than an architect in these years, and though he may have acted as a *cicerone* in Rome to visiting Englishmen, as has been suggested,[5] there is no indication that it was necessary for him to support himself by this profession. It is unknown where or how he picked up his knowledge of architectural drafting, which he is said (probably erroneously) to have passed on to Stuart,[6] and which made his presence invaluable on the expedition to Athens and later that to Ionia. Despite his secondary position, he won Stuart's praise for his intelligent and accurate delineation and measurements[7] as well as a place as second-in-command of the later Ionian expedition.

Both Hamilton at twenty-five and Revett at twenty-eight may have felt that their relative inexperience and youth did not equip them sufficiently to undertake this project without a more mature partner, for they discussed their plan, possibly on the Naples trip, with James Stuart

4. For Revett, see *AA*, IV, pp. xxviii–xxxi; *DNB*; John Nichols, *Literary Anecdotes of the Eighteenth Century*, London, 1817–1858, VI, p. 340, IX, pp. 147–148; *GM*, XLIX, July 1779, p. 374 (Ayot St. Lawrence); *GM*, LXXIV, Part 2, Nov. 1804, p. 860 (epitaph); *GM*, XCI, Part 2, Nov. 1821, p. 423 (biography); *Catalogue of the Library of N. Revett . . . Sold at Auction . . . June 26, 1804*; and Chapter II, note 41 below. There are a volume of Revett's drawings and a number of proof engravings at the Bodleian Library (Gough Misc. Ant. Fol. 4). John Harris has informed me that the RIBA Library owns a portrait of Revett holding Leonardo da Vinci's *Della Pittura* in his hand. For further information, see H. M. Colvin, *A Biographical Dictionary of English Architects 1660–1840*, London, 1954, pp. 493–495.

5. Lesley Lawrence, "Stuart and Revett: Their Literary and Architectural Careers", *JWCI*, II, July 1938, p. 130.

6. *GM*, LXIII, March 1788, p. 217 (critique on "Traits for the Life of the Late Athenian Stuart", which had appeared in *GM*, LXIII, Feb. 1788, pp. 95–96, 135–136, 181; and in *EM*, XIII, Feb. 1788, pp. 68–70, April 1788, pp. 284–285).

7. *AA*, I, pp. vii–viii.

(1713–1788), who at thirty-five was an older and more experienced man, and asked him to join them: by late 1748 Stuart had drawn up the first brief account of the proposed expedition.[8] Hamilton and Revett could not have made a better choice of a partner. Stuart had already demonstrated both his ability and his determination. Born the son of a Scottish mariner (presumably the eldest since he assumed responsibility for the care of the family), he was apprenticed to the fan-painter Louis Goupy,[9] and supported his mother, brother and two sisters from his work in this trade after the early death of his father. After the death of his mother he was able to set up his family in self-supporting positions in the fan-painting business, while he started out to fulfil what must have been a life-long ambition by travelling on foot to Rome. Along the way he paid his expenses by painting fans,[10] a trade which he may have continued practising in Italy, though he may also have acted as *cicerone* in Rome.[11] Before his travels he already had begun to improve himself by self-education, undertaking, for instance, the study of Latin in order to understand the captions under prints published after ancient masters.[12] He also probably had exhibited instances of his physical courage and endurance, as well as his ability to meet all kinds of people regardless of their social position, and to form enduring friendships; abilities which were the key to the success of the Athenian enterprise and to his own personal advancement. Early biographies of Stuart describe him as a self-made man, who rose from a lowly position without compromise to his integrity, "but by the bold

8. Appendix I, entry A.

9. John Harris has pointed out to me, if Stuart was apprenticed to Goupy, it is doubtful that he would have needed training as a draughtsman, since fan-painting demanded exquisite draughtsmanship.

10. "Memoires of Thomas Jones", *Walpole Society*, XXXII, 1946–1948, pp. 74–75: ". . . at one time he [Nulty] subsisted at *Venice* & other Cities as an itinerant Fan-painter, & if I recollect right, he told me that the late ingenious Mr Stewart (the *Athenian Stewart* as he was called) was his Associate in the same profession—however they were both very intimate, & pass'd through a great Variety of Scenes together—& he used to say that if it were not for fear of giving Offence to that Gentleman, & some other friends, he could have made a very entertaining history of their Adventures." Nulty later accompanied Robert Mylne to Sicily (see Appendix II, entries 160, 163, 164).

11. L. Lawrence, "Stuart and Revett", *JWCI*, II, July 1938, p. 130.

12. *GM*, LXIII, Feb. 1788, p. 95, where is also mentioned Stuart's interest in anatomy, drafting, geometry and mathematics, and it is suggested that he was encouraged by Goupy to improve himself.

efforts of unconquerable perseverance, prudence, and an independent mind".[13]

Stuart's reputation was advanced in Rome by two achievements. The first was his gaining of a reputation as a classical scholar. He studied at the Collegio di Propoganda Fide, and published a treatise in Latin which was said to have been the first scholarly work by a Protestant presented to the Pope.[14] Its dedication to the Earl of Malton, later the Marquess of Rockingham, an early patron and a life-long friend, is indicative of the second of his abilities: his talent at meeting wealthy and influential people with interests similar to his, and persuading them to support his enterprises. It has been said, erroneously, that Rockingham induced Stuart to embark on the Greek project.[15] Though this statement is unfounded, Rockingham was certainly one of Stuart's major patrons and doubtless helped to finance the Athenian expedition. Two other important contacts of Stuart in Rome were John Bouverie and James Dawkins, to whom he is said to have introduced himself after his arrival.[16] It is likely that Bouverie helped support Stuart, and it is certain that Dawkins not only patronized Stuart while he was in Rome, but made possible a lengthy extension of Stuart's and Revett's stay in Athens.[17] Later Dawkins received Stuart into his house in London, where Stuart may have remained

13. John Nichols, *Literary Anecdotes*, IX, p. 146. Apparently Stuart declined a knighthood (BM, MS Add. 27.576, p. 20). Always a person of integrity, even in later life, when his reputation for character had declined, he was chosen by Mrs Montagu for her architect "on account of his disinterestedness and contempt of money" (*Mrs. Montagu, "Queen of the Blues"*, ed. Reginald Blunt, London, 1923, II, pp. 82–83). For Stuart, see also *AA*, IV, pp. xxi–xxviii; *DNB; Chambers's Journal* XIII, 24 March 1860, pp. 179–181; H. M. Colvin, *Biographical Dictionary*, pp. 581–586; note 6 above; and Chapter II, notes 37, 39. Material relating to Stuart is preserved in the British Museum (MSS Add. 22.152, 22.153, 22.576): a Stuart notebook is in the Library of the RIBA. *Critical Observations on the Buildings of London*, London, 1771 and 1772 (reviewed *MR*, XLIV, April 1771, pp. 279–281), is attributed to Stuart; he wrote *A Discourse Delivered to the Students of the Royal Academy, on the Distribution of Prizes, 10 Dec. 1771* (reviewed *MR*, XLVI, May 1772, pp. 474–484); and reduced copies of his views for *AA*, I, were used by Alessandro Bisani in his *Picturesque Tour . . . by an Italian Gentleman*, London, 1793. Stuart is also responsible for the text of the *Antiquities of Athens*, vols. I, II, and for notes published in vols. III, IV.

14. *De Obelisco Caesaris Augusti, Campo Martis Nuperrime Effoso . . .* , 1751 (pub. in Latin and Italian): see *AA*, IV, p. xxvii.

15. James Mulvaney, *The Life of James Gandon*, Dublin, 1846, p. 197.

16. *GM*, LXIII, March 1788, p. 216.

17. *AA*, I, p. vi, note a. See also Appendix II, entry 4.

some time after Dawkins' death in 1759.[18] The last of Stuart's known patrons in Rome was Lord Charlemont, who remained in contact with Stuart in London through their mutual club, the Society of Dilettanti. All of these early patrons of the Greek trip were private individuals, interested in Greek antiquities as a matter of personal taste.

The fourth person to accompany Stuart, Revett and Hamilton to Naples in 1748 was Matthew Brettingham the younger (1725–1803), but he seems to have had little connection with the planning of the *Antiquities of Athens*.[19] Indeed, his main concern in Rome, a commission from his father to buy antiquities, did not place him in a position to consider seriously a trip to Greece. Though his position in relation to the conception of the Athenian publication is unknown,[20] Brettingham's connection with the Burlington circle through his father and his work at Holkham indicates, if only superficially, a link between the neo-Greek movement and the older Palladian revival. A more positive connection between the two was established by Stuart's first teacher, Louis Goupy; for Goupy accompanied Richard Boyle, Lord Burlington, on his first trip to Italy early in the century.[21] It has been suggested that Goupy was responsible for awakening Stuart's interest in antiquity.[22] But of course Stuart and Revett, as well as Hamilton and Brettingham, continued an English tradition of interest in antique sources of art as a means to improve taste, including

18. *GM*, LXIII, Feb. 1788, p. 96. However, L. Lawrence, "Stuart and Revett", *JWCI*, II, July 1938, p. 130, discounts this.

19. For Brettingham, see *DNB*; A. Michaelis, *Ancient Marbles in Great Britain*, Cambridge, 1882, pp. 71–73; Hugh Archibald Wyndham, *A Family History 1688–1837*; *The Wyndhams of Somerset, Sussex and Wiltshire*, London, 1950, p. 141, 169. Robert Adam commented to his brother James, 18 April 1755 (ERO, GD18/4770): ". . . it will require a very considerable interest to succeed against Chambers who has tollerable Friends & real merit, But still more to cutt out one Britingham who, has been 2 or 3 Years in Italy, has gone to England lately under great protection & has 15 or 20,000 £ from his Father, He had Commissions when in Rome for near £10,000 in statues, &ca. But the only comfort & hopes of his not being invincible is from his Genius being much inferiour to his Fortune".

20. Brettingham remained in contact with both Stuart and Revett: letters (now lost) of some importance, though not concerning the *Antiquities*, from him to Stuart after Stuart had left Rome, are mentioned in *AA*, IV, p. iii. Apparently Stuart also corresponded with Brettingham about the progress of their investigations (see Appendix II, entry 4).

21. Horace Walpole, *Anecdotes of Painting*, ed. Warnam, London, 1876, III, p. 32.

22. H. M. Colvin, work cited in note 4 above, p. 581.

both concern with Palladio's modern interpretations of ancient architecture and with collecting antique art.

Although Stuart stated in the *Antiquities* that toward the end of 1748 he "first drew up a brief account of our motives for undertaking this work, of the form we proposed to give it, and of the subject which we then hoped to compose it",[23] the first recorded mention of the project is found in the previously-mentioned letter from Revett to his father dated 6 January 1749.[24] The ambition of the authors regarding the scope of the work, their optimism about the amount of time to complete it and the financial gains to expect, are reflected in Revett's estimation that the work would be published within four years (of which only one year would be spent in Greece), and that it would net them a minimum profit of £10,000. Revett continued in this strain of optimism in a later letter concerning their pending departure from Rome on 17 December 1749, three months before it actually took place.[25]

Hamilton probably was with Stuart and Revett in Rome during the preparatory phase of the expedition; apparently he lived with them after their return from Naples,[26] and thus may still have considered accompanying them to Athens. However, at some time before they left for Venice on the first leg of their trip he decided to drop out of the project. His character does not seem to have been suited to the sustained and concentrated interest which the project demanded.[27] After Hamilton withdrew, the youthful enthusiasm with which the expedition was conceived ended, and the venture began to become practical. Problems arose in the original planning; the hope of large-scale profits dwindled; calculations of the amount of time and the risks incurred grew; and, above all, it became necessary to find a new type of backer—people who could help

23. Appendix I, entry A.
24. Appendix I, entry B.
25. *AA*, IV, p. xxx.
26. U. Thieme and F. Becker, *Allgemeines Lexikon der bildenden Künstler . . .*, Leipzig, 1907–1947. XV, p. 552.
27. For Hamilton's character, see Edward Edwards, *Anecdotes of Painters*, London, 1808, p. 256: "He [Hamilton] was a man of very pleasant manners and respectable character, but not calculated to pursue the study of his art with that vigour that is necessary to the attainment of great excellence."

the two men raise a subscription that would give them increased funds
and an assurance of wide-scale support.

When they arrived in Venice in March–April 1750, Stuart and Revett
began to interest influential people in their project, and to collect subscriptions for the eventual publication.[28] The patrons they now sought
were of a different character from those in Rome. In Venice they were
aided by practical career men, who introduced the two partners to a
wider circle of interested subscribers and smoothed the way for the trip to
Greece. Chief among these were Sir James Gray, British Resident in
Venice, and Joseph Smith, British Consul in Venice. Stuart stated that Sir
James Gray was the "first to set on foot a Subscription for our intended
Work",[29] and he also may have been responsible for taking the project
out of the realm of fancy and putting it on a firm financial ground. In
addition, Gray introduced them to the Society of Dilettanti, and in 1751
proposed their names for membership, thus making them the first artists
to become members of this society. Composed of wealthy and socially
prominent men, forming a self-stated link between English society and
English dilettanti in Italy, the Society was ideally suited to promote the
work of Stuart and Revett. It is certain that Gray's nomination of the two
men was made with the intention of securing further support for their
project through enlarging the scope of their patronage. Their other
major Venetian patron, Joseph Smith, arranged for their protection while
in Greece through Sir James Porter, Ambassador at Constantinople.
Smith and Porter were also members of the Society of Dilettanti, and
along with Gray heralded the future involvement of this Society not only
with the *Antiquities of Athens* but also with many later projects concerned
with the Levant.[30]

28. Appendix I, entry C, letter introducing the 1751 Proposal.   29. *AA*, I, p. vi.

30. Among its publications, the Society of Dilettanti was responsible not only for the *AA*
volumes, but also for *The Antiquities of Ionia*, 1769–1915, 5v.; Richard Payne Knight, *An Account of
the Worship of Priapus*, 1786; Richard Chandler, *Inscriptiones antiquae* (1774), *Travels in Asia Minor*
(1775), *Travels in Greece* (1776); *Select Specimens of Ancient Sculpture*, 1809–1835, 2 v.; *The Unedited
Antiquities of Attica*, 1817; Sir William Gell, *Rome and Its Vicinity*, 1834; R. P. Knight, *An Inquiry
into the Symbolical Language of Ancient Art and Mythology*, 1818 (reprinted 1835); P. O. Brönsted,
The Bronzes of Siris, 1836; F. C. Penrose, *Two Letters from Athens* (1847), *An Investigation of the
Principles of Athenian Architecture* (1851).

While waiting in Venice for a ship to take them to their eventual destination, Stuart and Revett made a trip to Pola. From July to November 1750 they measured the antique monuments there, doubtless with the idea of having something concrete to show prospective subscribers. There is an early scheme, now lost, to include the antiquities at Pola in volume two of their work.[31] The first preserved proposal for the *Antiquities* dates after their return from Pola. Although it embodies the essence, and in many instances the wording, of all the known proposals, and was used to enlist support for the project, it does not appear to have existed outside of manuscript form, and is known to us only through a letter by Thomas Hollis to Professor John Ward describing its contents.[32] Fortunately, Hollis felt that the manuscript was important enough to merit his copying its entire contents into his letter.

In the proposal preserved in Hollis' letter, the publication was described as intended for connoisseurs and dilettanti of English society, "lovers of polite literature", who were equally concerned with the history, the great men, and the antiquities of Athens. Thus, from the outset the publication was designed for readers who would be more interested in concepts of taste than in technical architectural problems. Indeed, the publication was probably not intended to supply models for architects, but to provide examples of taste for amateurs.[33] Stuart's justification of the work as satisfying curiosity and improving taste reaffirmed this interpretation, in spite of the fact that in this early proposal he followed a traditional precedent of attributing a double function to the archaeological publication: it was to serve not only lovers of antiquity but also artists, who would now be better instructed by drawing their examples nearer to the "fountain head" of art.

Tribute then was paid to the ancient theory of the primacy of Greek art and its use as a source for the later art of civilized and cultured nations: Rome was considered to have borrowed her arts from Greece. But, the

31. Appendix I, entry GI.
32. Appendix I, entry C.
33. For the intended readers of the archaeological publications, see, for instance, Appendix II, entries 12, 104, 105, and 155.

proposal went on, while the arts of Rome were recorded visually by architects and artists, and distributed throughout the polite nations of Europe, those of Athens had been entirely neglected. Stuart claimed that none of the previous travellers to Athens, who were more concerned with literature than with the arts, had made a professional survey of Greek monuments, that is, with "accurate measurements and attentive delineation". One of the major justifications for the publication was, then, the recording of Athenian monuments, which Stuart felt would be lost to the world if they were not preserved in this fashion.

Having established the purpose of the publication, Stuart moved to its contents. The work was to be divided into three volumes—the first to consist of views, the second of architectural reconstructions accurately measured after the manner of Desgodets, and the third of sculpture. Architectural subjects were chosen by consulting ancient authors and interviewing recent travellers to Greece. But the scope of the work was not confined to accurate delineation since the monuments were to be supported with detailed explanations pointing out their relation to Vitruvius' doctrine and the description of ancient writers, such as Pausanias, Strabo, etc. In other words, this ambitious publication would combine the functions of an archaeological study and an architectural treatise. Moreover, this project would go even beyond Desgodets. Now there would be a wider assortment of examples of ancient architecture so that a truer picture of it might be formed than could be done from the work of the French architect, who, Stuart claimed, was deficient in examples of the Doric and Ionic Orders.

It can be assumed from Stuart's discussion of the proposals[34] that those issued up to 1755 were similar to the one issued in Venice. However, a change can be observed. The material, which in the first proposal was arranged by volume according to views, architecture and sculpture, in the known later proposals was arranged by volume according to geographical location, and within each volume by individual monument. The

34. *AA*, I, p. vi, note a.

work thus developed from a categorical report on antiquity to a comprehensive study of single works.

Stuart and Revett left Venice for Greece on 19 January 1751. They
travelled economically in stages on ships that happened to be available,
and headed toward their destination.[35] They stopped at Patras (22–26
February) and Corinth (28 February–c. 16 March), where they measured
the temple and sketched views while waiting for their ship. They did not
reach Athens, where they made their headquarters, until 18 March. They
seem to have spent the greater portion of their time in this city, and only
went on two expeditions: in May 1751 with Wood and Dawkins through
the mainland of Greece where they saw Delphi and revisited Corinth, and
from 5 March to c. 18 June 1753 to Smyrna and Delos while escaping
danger at Athens due to political upheaval.[36] Interrupted by the plague
and political unrest, the work at Athens had to be abandoned unfinished
toward the end of 1753. Stuart left Athens on 20 September, and with his
departure this stage of the project came to a close.

Thus, for almost three years the two architects concentrated on measuring the ruins of Athens. That their work remained incomplete after this
length of time may have been due to their method of procedure, which
was time-consuming and painstaking, though not completely without
errors.[37] A famous example of the extraordinary thoroughness with which
the work was done is that of the house they had torn down and rebuilt in
order to measure the Tower of the Winds. However, both Stuart and
Revett may have been inclined to interests beyond those of the work
stipulated in their proposals, which kept them from concentrating on
their main task. A letter addressed to Revett charges him with obtaining
the answers to a long list of miscellaneous questions,[38] while Stuart is

35. In contrast, Charlemont and Dawkins had private ships specially fitted out for them (see
Chapter II, note 12, for Charlemont; see *Palmyra*, pp. a r and a v, for Dawkins).
36. *AA*, IV, pp. iv–xvii, quoting from a journal by Stuart.
37. See Jacob Landy, "Stuart and Revett: Pioneer Archaeologists", *Archaeology*, IX, Dec. 1956,
pp. 252–259.
38. *AA*, IV, p. iii.

known to have had many irons in the fire.[39] Although a later *Antiquities* editor claimed that papers in his possession refute the story, it was rumoured that Stuart had at some time during his stay in Greece served voluntarily as chief engineer in the Hungarian army.[40]

Revett left Athens on 27 January 1754 and met Stuart, who had faced many hazards,[41] at Salonica on 20 April 1754. He had missed the next Athenian archaeologist, Julien-David LeRoy,[42] by several months. LeRoy was in Venice a month before he left for Greece on 5 May 1754, but he stopped only momentarily in Attica before going on to Constantinople to get permission for his investigations. He did not return to Athens until 1 February 1755 when, pleased with the co-operation of both Turks and Greeks—in contrast to the experience of Stuart and Revett, whose meticulous methods caused them to be regarded as spies— he succeeded in observing and measuring all the major monuments of Athens in less than three months.[43]

Meanwhile, at Negropont, in a letter, now lost,[44] Stuart and Revett reappraised the work they had done and the amount they could hope to accomplish. This letter stated the intention of the authors to publish only the Lantern of Demosthenes (Monument of Lysicrates) and the Tower of the Winds in a first volume of the *Antiquities*, and then to return to Athens, after the political unrest had ended, to complete the measurements of the other buildings prior to further publication. From this communication we can assume that only these two monuments were measured and drawn up with the thoroughness that the two authors required (though Stuart

39. See *GM*, LXIII, Feb. 1788, pp. 95–96, and a list of projects begun by Stuart in BM, MS Add. 22.152.

40. *AA*, IV, p. xvii. *GM*, LXIII, Feb. 1788, p. 96, is the source for the rumour.

41. Andrew Caldwell, "An Account of the Extraordinary Escape of James Stewart, from being Put to Death by Some Turks in Whose Company He Happened to be Travelling", *EM*, XLVI, Nov. 1804, pp. 369–371.

42. For LeRoy, see M. A. Dacier, "Notice historique sur la vie et les ouvrages de M. Julien-David Leroy", (read 23 March 1804), *Mémoires de l'institut royal de France: classe d'histoire et de littérature ancienne*, Paris, N.S. (1815), I, pp. 267–284: summarized in René Dussaud, *La nouvelle Académie des Inscriptions et Belles Lettres (1795–1914)*, Paris, 1946, I, pp. 82–83.

43. *Les Antiquités d'Athènes*, Paris, 1808, I, p. ix, n. 1: "Il . . . y [at Athens] resta à peine autant de mois que les deux voyageurs anglais y avaient passé d'années."

44. Appendix I, entry I.

later stated that only the Propylaea and the Arch of Hadrian remained to be measured when they left Athens[45]). At any rate, the end of two and a half years of work on the site did not produce a finished project, and the outcome was a set of miscellaneous sheets, most of which appeared eventually in later volumes of the *Antiquities*. The men seem to have been unable to translate their original project into reality. Possibly it could never have been realized practically: it was, as it were, a dream of the ultimate solution to the architectural treatise, in which the essential qualities of architecture were to be re-discovered through meticulous reporting on the architectural remains of Greece; it looked backwards to the Renaissance and forward to the scientific world to come.

The rest of the voyage of these two men was anticlimactic. They again visited the Greek archipelago and Delos, where they completed their observations, stayed at Andros six weeks, partly because of reports of the plague at Smyrna, left Smyrna on 6 September 1754 for Marseilles, and returned to England on 27 October 1754. Already by the time they returned their project was no longer exclusive, for Wood had published his *Ruins of Palmyra* in November of the preceding year.

In January of 1755 the final proposal was published, which probably described the reduced contents of their final scheme.[46] This proposal was an enlargement of the idea suggested at Negropont of presenting several minor monuments, to include, along with a general view of Athens, five examples.[47] Illustrations of the Tower of the Winds and the Monument

45. *AA*, II, p. 37.
46. Appendix I, entry J.
47.

Contents of First Volume of AA	Views	Architecture	Sculpture	Misc.
General View of Athens	1			
A Doric Portico at Athens	1	5		
The Ionic Temple on the Ilissus	1	7		
The Octago Tower of Andronicus Cyrrhestes	1	8	8	2
The Choragic Monument of Lysicrates, commonly called the Lanthorn of Demosthenes	1	8	17	
A Stoa or Portico, commonly supposed to be the remains of the Temple of Jupiter Olympus	1	10		
	6	38	25	2

of Lysicrates, the most complete of all their studies, may have been issued with this final proposal; Barthélemy mentioned seeing some finished plates in this year,[48] and three years later Robert Adam referred to these two monuments.[49] Also during 1755 they decided not to do the engraving themselves, and hired two engravers.[50]

The *Antiquities* was mentioned only intermittently now—a comment in a letter, or a joke on the time needed for publication.[51] Meanwhile, Stuart was busy making contacts in order to get architectural and painting commissions, and he secured several sizeable jobs as well as (in 1758) the permanent position of Surveyor to Greenwich Hospital,[52] while Revett probably drifted back to the life of country gentleman to which he had been bred. Thus procrastination and outside interests doubtless contributed to the delay in publishing the *Antiquities of Athens*, as they had to the gathering of the original material.

Whatever the external causes for the delay in publication, in the final analysis the fault must lie with Stuart and Revett. They had been in Greece three years compared to LeRoy's less than three months and Wood's nine days in both Palmyra and Balbec.[53] Even Desgodets, their model, had spent only sixteen months working in Rome, and had come back with twice as much material as he published. They had arrived in England one year after the publication of *Palmyra*, which provided a fine introduction for their work, and two years before the publication of *Balbec*. LeRoy did not return to Europe until almost half a year after Stuart and Revett. Yet within a year he had published a proposal describing an ambitious project, which included the major monuments of Greece, divided into historical and architectural sections, and a dis-

48. Appendix II, entry 85.
49. Appendix II, entry 90.
50. The engravers hired were Robert Strange and James Basire (Appendix II, entry 102). Only Basire seems to have remained with the publication (Appendix II, entry 90). The other engravers were E. Rooker and A. Walker: the vignettes were by J. Couse.
51. Appendix II, entries 86–99.
52. See Lesley Lewis, "The Architects of the Chapel at Greenwich Hospital", *AB*, XXIX, Dec. 1947, pp. 260–267.
53. For the timing of Wood's trip, see Chapter II, note 49.

course on the principles of architecture.[54] Stuart and Revett must have been aware of this proposal (it should be considered that the relationship of each publication to the works preceding it was of such concern that, for instance, Adam delayed his publication of Spalato, even though it was not concerned with Greek architecture, by several years after the *Antiquities of Athens* appeared in order to ensure its success[55]), but they did not act on their knowledge, with the result that the *Ruines* appeared some four years before the *Antiquities*.

Stuart's foreword to the *Antiquities*, in which he cited the text of the proposal as it had existed in its first form and alleged that LeRoy adopted it for his work,[56] may have indicated an even further change in plans due to the latter's publication. And, to be sure, the eventual publication of the *Antiquities* must be understood partly as a reaction to LeRoy's *Ruines*. The text was the antithesis of that of LeRoy's work: a comparison of the terse, informative passages of the *Antiquities* with LeRoy's comments marks the difference between the two. Stuart, writing of the "Lanthorn of Demosthenes", said:

> This Monument of Antiquity, which is exquisitely wrought, stands near the eastern end of the Acropolis and is partly enclosed in the Hospitium of the Capuchins. It is composed of three distinct parts. First, a quadrangular Basement; secondly, a circular Colonnade, the

54. Appendix I, entry K; Appendix II, entries 30, 31. A revised English edition of LeRoy's *Ruines* was issued by Robert Sayer in the year following its French publication (see Chapter III, note 22): an abbreviated German edition of Sayer was published in 1764 by Georg Christoph Kilian, who also published an edition of Balbec in 1769.

55. See John Fleming, "The Journey to Spalato", from "An Adam Miscellany", AR, CXXIII, Feb. 1958, pp. 103–107; and Appendix II, entries 93, 99.

56. AA, I, p. vi, note a: "We must here observe that Mons. Le Roy was at Rome in the year 1748, when our first Scheme of this Work appeared there, and soon became very generally a Topic of discourse, among the men of curiosity and learning in that City; and when he read the description of Palmyra, which he has cited, he must have known that we had already employed ourselves for some time at Athens, in the execution of our Scheme. Now by his own account he did not resolve on a journey to Greece till 1753, nor set out from Venice, till May 5, 1754; which is more than a Year, after the last publication of our Scheme dated from Athens, was printed at Venice by Consul Smith. . . . whatever motives of improvement to himself, or glory to his country, Mons. Le Roy has thought it proper to assigne, for his resolution of visiting Greece, and designing the Antiquities there; he seems to have formed it, in consequence of our having first undertaken the same Task." Certainly by 1754 LeRoy was aware of the Stuart-Revett project (see Appendix II, entry 83).

intercolumniations of which were entirely closed up; and thirdly, a *Tholus* or Cupola with the Ornament which is placed on it.[57]

LeRoy, on the other hand, remarked:

> Ce monument est, comme on le voit, engagé dans une mauvaise maison; c'est l'Hospice des Capuchins d'Athènes: le R. P. Agathanage en étoit supérieur quand je passai dans cette ville. J'ai reçu de ce Religieux toutes sortes d'honnêtés; il a trouvé le secret de se faire aimer & respecter de toutes les personnes de notre nation qui ont occasion de le voir leur commerce, ainsi que des Turcs & des Grecs.
>
> La Porte ronde percée dans un mur, qui est à gauche dans la Vue, est l'entrée de son Couvent: elle est couronnée par les armes de France, que ce Religieux, aussi bon François que bon Catholique y a fait mettre. Les maisons que l'on voit à droite forment l'autre côté de la rue. J'ai cru qu'on ne seroit pas fâché qu'en représentant la Lanterne de Démosthène, je représentasse aussi une danse des Grecs assez curieuse que je vis dans le temps du carnaval, quand je dessinois cet édifice. Voici comme ils exécutent cette danse. . . .[58]

and concluded that this dance originated with Theseus. Later, because of a misinterpretation of the figures in the frieze, LeRoy renamed the "Lantern" a Temple of Hercules.

A major portion of the first volume of the *Antiquities* is devoted to a refutation of LeRoy. Stuart's comments on the *Ruines* summed up the situation as pithily as his descriptions summed up the ancient buildings. He said that LeRoy's mistakes "have most of them been made before, tho' in fewer Words, by Wheler and Spon; none of them are perhaps so pleasant as Mons. LeRoy's change of the Dolphins into dead Men",[59] and observed that: "The Fact seems to be, that Mons. LeRoy had heard, and perhaps read, of both these Churches [the Ionic Temple of the Ilissus

57. *AA*, I, p. 27.

58. *Ruines*, 1758, p. 25.

59. *AA*, I, p. 35. This, although Dalton had clearly shown dolphins in his *Musaeum Graecum* illustration of the frieze.

and the Temple of Diana Agrotera], but in Reality has seen neither of them: and his Account happens to be confused, because he has unluckily joined the two Relations together, and has attributed them both to one Building".[60] Stuart's comments on the Stoa or Portico at Athens are too long to be included here,[61] but his exposition of LeRoy's errors and their sources is masterly.

Though Stuart's sarcasm may have been due in part to his ire at having his own plans ruined by another publication, and one which owed its conception to his proposal, it must also have been due to the annoyance of a student of antiquity and a scholar on seeing the work of an amateur, and a rather poor amateur at that, working in the field which he regarded as his own immediate and major speciality. It was as a professional that he criticized LeRoy when he said that: "the study of Architecture which he [LeRoy] professes, the critical knowledge which he affects to display in that Art, the appearance of precision in his Measures, and the pompous circumstances of his Publication, give an air of Authenticity to his Errors, which seems perfectly calculated to impose them on us for so many accurate Truths".[62] He justified his insistence on accuracy by citing Desgodets, who even corrected Palladio and Serlio in his work.[63]

It has been suggested that the original broad scope of the publication was abandoned in favour of illustrations of ornament for architectural use, in order to capitalize on the popularity of "Gusto Greco" ornament in the 1760s.[64] To be sure, Stuart does state that he intended to emphasize the Orders as the "different Grecian modes of decorating Buildings" in his preface to the second volume of the *Antiquities*. However, it would be a mistake to think of these Orders as merely ornamental features of a building. The Orders had formed the solid backbone to architectural theory and practice since the Renaissance, and it was certainly in this light that Stuart thought of them. One of the major motives of the original proposal was the desire of Stuart and Revett to acquaint the interested public with the true state of ancient architecture through a fairly repre-

60. *AA*, I, p. 11. 61. *Ibid.*, pp. 44–52. 62. *Ibid.*, p. 52. 63. *Ibid.*
64. L. Lawrence, article cited in note 5 above, p. 131; H. M. Colvin, *Biographical Dictionary*, London, 1954, p. 582.

sentative group of examples of the ancient Orders: examples which they felt that even Desgodets, the only previous authority on ancient architecture to use this method, lacked. From this goal they never deviated.

Moreover, Stuart and Revett could not have considered profit as a motive for the modification of the format of the *Antiquities* to contemporaneous taste. Hope of capitalizing commercially on a trend in taste must have dwindled away long before the decision was made to change the programme of the publication. Not only would the expenses of Wood's two volumes have been known, but it is possible that their own subscription money was not sufficient to meet current bills, for the Society of Dilettanti contributed money toward the volume,[65] as did private individuals.[66] Nor would Stuart have benefited from the fame that the work was to bring him since he had established himself already and received his most important commissions before the work was published. And, finally, the work was not intended for the use of architects. Its price alone rendered such a function prohibitive; it was not until the nineteenth century that French and English editions brought down the price enough to make the *Antiquities* generally available.[67] There are only

65. Lionel Cust, *History of the Society of Dilettanti*, ed. Sydney Colvin, London, 1898, p. 80: twenty guineas was given by the Society in 1757 "for further Encouragement of so great and useful a Work". The Society also proposed donating a like sum for each additional volume. The work hardly paid the expenses arising from its prosecution, according to *AA*, IV, p. xxx.

66. *AA*, I, p. vi, note a: Stuart mentioned obligations to Colonel George Gray that would only be due to his financial support of the publication, and stated that ". . . the generosity of some Persons of the highest Distinction, had prevented it [Dawkins' death] from affecting in the least, the Publication of our Work. It were too great a sacrifice to delicacy, should we forbear to mention the obligations they have bestowed on us, tho' at the same time, we have reason to believe, they would be better pleased in having these also, as well as their names, passed over in silence."

67. *Les Antiquités d'Athènes*, ed. C. P. Landon, Paris, 1808, I, pp. v–vi: "L'importance de ce bel ouvrage et le temps qui s'est écoulé depuis qu'on en a publiée la première partie: son excessive rareté en France, où nos plus vastes bibliothèques en présentent à peine quelques exemplaires incomplets, et où l'on n'a que des notions imparfaites de son but et de sa composition; sa destinée singulière qui fait qu'après tant d'années, après la mort de presque tous ceux qui y ont successivement coopéré, il est encore pour l'Angleterre elle-même un livre en quelque sort nouveau . . ."; and *AA*, ed. W. Kinnard, London, 1825, I, p. 3: ". . . we have long felt the utility and necessity of the production of a correct and perfect Edition, more suitable to the means of the Antiquarian, the Architect, the Student, the Builder, and the Artificer, and at the same time not to be found unworthy the attention of the Amateur. The Edition hitherto known in England is from its costliness scarcely ever seen in private libraries, and rarely to be found perfect in that of the professional architect". For prices of the archaeological publications, see Chapter III, note 28.

C

four architects and three builders out of a total of over 500 subscribers to the first volume,[68] and contemporaries interested in the publication did not mention its use by architects. This work, as well as other archaeological publications of the time, went to wealthy and socially prominent dilettanti and connoisseurs. The new taste which arose within this group of patrons was one of the major routes through which archaeology would be introduced into architecture.

Prior to the nineteenth century the importance of the *Antiquities of Athens* depended mainly on the first volume: after its publication Revett sold his interest in the work to Stuart.[69] The next volume did not appear until 1789, long after archaeological publications had become the vogue, and, indeed, even after Stuart's death. A proposal for the third volume, mentioned in Stuart's preface to the second volume, introduced a new arrangement. However, the proposal was not carried out. The second volume lacked the coherence of the first, being compiled from Stuart's notes, original drawings, plates previously made (probably intended for the originally projected first volume) and special plates made by the Society of Dilettanti. The defects of this volume were augmented in volumes three and four, published in 1794 and 1816, and the final volume, published as a supplement in 1830, had hardly more than its name in common with the original enterprise of Stuart and Revett.[70]

68. A complete list of *AA* subscribers is in the Soane Museum copy of this work.

69. Adolf Michaelis, "Die Gesellschaft der Dilettanti in London", *Zeitschrift für bildende Kunst*, XIV, 1879, p. 135. However, L. Lawrence, article cited in note 5, p. 131, and H. M. Colvin, *Biographical Dictionary*, London, 1954, p. 582, say Revett sold out to Stuart before *AA*, I, was published.

70. In addition to C. R. Cockerell, *The Antiquities of Athens and Other Places of Greece, Sicily, etc.*, London, 1830, several other supplements to the *AA* appeared: J. G. Legrand, *Monumens de la Grèce*, Paris, 1808; William Wilkins, *Atheniensia*, London, 1816; H. W. Inwood, *The Erechtheion at Athens*, London, 1827.

CHAPTER II

Expeditions, Tourists, Patrons and Publications

THREE voyages to the Levant of the 1670s provide much of the background for later publications concerned with Greece, and foreshadow some of the characteristics of later expeditions. Each of them had its own character, orientation, and method of recording what was found. The first of these voyages was made in 1674 by the Comte de Nointel, French Ambassador to Constantinople. (Stuart spoke of him as the first person of any consequence to go to Greece.[1]) Nointel's expedition was carried out with all the pomp and circumstance to which he, as a member of the court of Louis XIV, was entitled. Included in his large retinue were a classical scholar and two artists. But in spite of the desire for scholarship and for the recording of the ancient monuments that these additions to his party presuppose, little of archaeological value resulted from this voyage, except for Carrey's record of the Parthenon sculptures.[2]

The next expedition was made in 1675 by the Englishmen Francis Vernon and Sir Giles Eastcourt. (Stuart noted that of the early travellers Vernon was the most diligent.[3]) Vernon, a veteran traveller, was also an astronomer and mathematician. His interests extended to architecture, and in spite of "brutishly barbarous" Turks, he claimed to have been able to

1. *AA*, III, "On the Plan of Athens", p. ii.
2. However, Nointel's interest in the notes on Greece made by the Père J. P. Babin, which he sent to Lyon, may have caused Spon to undertake his trip to the Levant: see R. D. Middleton, "The Abbé de Cordemoy and the Graeco-Gothic Ideal: A Prelude to Romantic Classicism", *JWCI*, XXV, July–Dec. 1962, p. 286.
3. *AA*, III, "On the Plan of Athens", p. ii.

maintain a discrepancy of no more than half a foot in his measurements of
the Temple of Minerva in Athens. His sense of adventure and his interest
in accurate reportage reflect an English approach to antiquity which was
promoted by the Royal Society; the *Philosophical Transactions*, the
journal of the Society, published an account of his travels.[4]

The outstanding expedition to Greece of this group, and the one most
influential for later travel to Greece, was that made by Jacob Spon and Sir
George Wheler in 1676. (Stuart referred to them as the most persevering
of the early travellers.[5]) If Nointel represented official French interest, and
Vernon the English adventurer, Spon represented the French antiquarian, lacking official patronage but with an international antiquarian
tradition behind him. Spon's careful notes and co-ordination of facts
with those mentioned by classical authors caused him to become the outstanding authority on Greece for later writers:[6] both Stuart and LeRoy
referred to Spon continually in their publications. But Wheler, a botanist
rather than a classical scholar, did not contribute anything of antiquarian
or archaeological importance in his work,[7] and even Spon's work was
that of a collector, compiler and scientific observer, rather than of an
artist or an architect. However, this expedition, probably in combination
with that of Nointel and other less important observers and writers on
Greece, was responsible for the idea (presented in 1696 though never
carried out) of sending French architectural students to study in Greece.[8]
It is at this point that Greek archaeology may have been connected for the
first time directly with architectural theory and training.

After these seventeenth-century journeys there was a lull in voyages to
the Levant. In the 1730s expeditions again were resumed, but now as

4. Letter to Oldenburg, 10 Jan. 1675, published in *Philosophical Transactions*, 1676; and in *AA*,
III, pp. 3–5, note a. Also see Bernard Randolph, *The Present State of the Morea*, London, 1689 (3rd
ed.), p. 14.

5. *AA*, III, "On the Plan of Athens", p. ii.

6. Jacob Spon, *Voyage d'Italie, de Dalmatie, de Grèce et du Levant*, Lyon, 1678.

7. George Wheler, *A Journey into Greece*, London, 1682 (French trans., Amsterdam, 1689).

8. *CD*, II, pp. 253–254, Marquis de LaTeulière to A. Villacerf, 9 August 1698. Alfred Maury, *Les
Académies d'autrefois*, II; *L'Ancienne Académie des Inscriptions et Belles-Lettres*, Paris, 1864, p. 221, men-
tions that Peyssonnel, a French diplomatic agent in the Levant in the 1740s, urged the Académie des
Inscriptions et Belles-Lettres to promote archaeological studies in Greece.

ventures of private English gentlemen. These new voyages still incorporated elements of the seventeenth-century tours: on-the-spot drawing, classical literary scholarship, precise measurements, antiquarian interests, and love of adventure. It was with members of this group, such as Richard Pococke, John Rawdon and Robert Wood,[9] that Stuart and Revett could have been in contact when seeking advice for their own pending trip. For our purposes, since it was concerned partly with architecture and was undertaken by future members of the Society of Dilettanti, the most important recorded tour to the Levant before the first *Antiquities* proposal was the 1738 voyage of John Montague, Earl of Sandwich, undertaken with his tutor the Rev. J. Cooke, William Ponsonby (later Earl of Bessborough), the Messrs Nelthorpe and (Sir) John Mackye, and the painter Jean-Etienne Liotard.[10] They covered the Eastern end of the Mediterranean, including Athens, collected both sculpture and inscriptions, made plans of the ancient monuments, and apparently were interested, as Vernon had been, in accurate measurements. Sandwich's journal indicates that they encountered a difficulty similar to that of Vernon: they were unable to make accurate measurements of the Parthenon because the Turks were afraid that they were measuring the fortifications.[11]

This older tradition of travel in the Levant still was dominant in the first expedition undertaken after the 1748 proposal, and made by one of Stuart's earliest patrons, James Caulfeild, Earl of Charlemont, together with Mr Francis Pierpont Burton (later Lord Coyningham), the Messrs Scott and Murphy, and the artist Richard Dalton, who joined them en

9. Richard Pococke, Bishop of Meath, was in the Levant between 1736–1740: he wrote *A Description of the East*, London, 1743–1745, and *Inscriptionum antiquarum*, London, 1752. John Rawdon, Earl of Moira, travelled to Greece and the East sometime before his election to the Society of Dilettanti in 1741. Wood was in the Levant twice in the early 1740s (see *DNB* and note 50 below). Also travelling at this time were Charles Perry, who wrote *A View of the Levant . . .*, London, 1743; and Alexander Drummond, *Travels through Different Cities of . . . Greece . . .*, London, 1754.

10. See John Montague, Fourth Earl of Sandwich, *A Voyage Performed by the Late Earl of Sandwich Round the Mediterranean in the Years 1738 and 1739*, London, 1799: Preface by the Rev. J. Cooke.

11. *Ibid.*, p. 63.

route.[12] Charlemont had left the University of Turin for Rome in 1748, and must have had conversations in Rome with Stuart and Revett before he set sail in April 1749. Indeed, in the small and tightly-knit English colony at Rome, the Athenian venture was undoubtedly a lively topic of conversation. But Charlemont's trip still recalled Sandwich's earlier one: the all-inclusive character; the interest in a collection of miscellaneous data, such as measurements;[13] and the lack of provision for publication of the findings, do not demonstrate yet a concentrated and scholarly interest in specific elements of the classical past. Dalton's later publications (*Views of Places . . . in . . . Asia Minor, Remarks on . . . the Present Inhabitants of Egypt*, and *Musaeum Graecum*)[14] are evidence of his attempt to profit from the trip rather than of a premeditated plan before the voyage, which he joined only after it had begun, and on impulse. The crude draughtsmanship and lack of detail of Dalton's engravings demonstrate that they were not intended for the instruction of scholars, architects, dilettanti, or even the public in general. Their value was probably as souvenirs. Dalton was concerned only with his personal advantages from the publication: in order to set himself up as an authority he wished to challenge even Wood's scholarship, and attempted to bill members of Charlemont's party twice for subscriptions to his work.[15]

12. *GM*, LXIX, March 1791, p. 195: "The whole of the voyage was not premeditated by the Editor [Dalton], but owing to mere chance. An invitation was given him by Sir Roger Kynaston, esq, of Shrewsbury, in company with Mr (afterwards Sir John) Frederick, with the intention only to accompany them . . . to Catania, where they met with Lord Charlemont, Mr Burton, now Lord Cunningham [*sic*], with Mr Scott and the late Mr Murphy. This party all sailed together in a ship, hired by Mr Charlemont and his party from Leghorn, with the intention of making that voyage: . . . [Dalton] was prevailed on to accompany [them] . . . and made the voyage to Constantinople, several parts of Greece, and Egypt, which he described in the best manner, by publishing prints after correct drawings as before mentioned." For Charlemont, see M. J. Craig, *The Volunteer Earl. Being the Life and Times of James Caulfeild, the First Earl of Charlemont*, London, 1948; Henry Grattan, *Memoires of Grattan*, London, 1839–1846, 5v.; Francis Hardy, *Memoires of the Political and Private Life of James Caulfield*, [*sic*] *Earl of Charlemont*, London, 1812 (2nd ed.); *The Manuscripts and Correspondence of James, First Earl of Charlemont*, London, 1891–1894 (*Historical Manuscripts Commission*, 12th Report, Appendix, Part X, I; 13th Report, Appendix, Part VIII, II).

13. Charlemont to R. Marlay, 6 September 1749 (H. Grattan, *Memoires*, II, p. 112): "I have been very busy measuring a column, above one hundred feet high, which is of one stone . . ."

14. For Dalton's work see Johann Fiorillo, *Geschichte der zeichnenden Künst . . .*, Göttingen, 1798–1808, V, p. 641, notes 2, 3; and *GM*, LXI, Part 1, March 1791, pp. 195–196.

15. T. Adderly to Charlemont, 28 January 1755 (*Manuscripts and Correspondence of Charlemont*,

Little is known at present about the crucial events of the 1740s in Rome, less about their relationship to interest in the Levant. But it is certain that one major cause of the sudden outburst of travel in the Eastern Mediterranean was the atmosphere created by the Grand Tour and the character of the English tourist who embarked on it. If the Grand Tour resulted from the desire of the English to compete culturally with the Continent, and was formed around Shaftesbury's aesthetic and Richardson's guide,[16] by the middle of the eighteenth century it had acquired a character that was broader, more superficial, and in many cases directly opposed to its original aims. A contemporary description satirized the average Grand Tourist of the period with these words:

> . . . an *English* youth & an *English* tutor on their travels are usually distinguished by the name of the bear and the bear leader, a disgrace which we have incurred by the ridiculous custom of sending our youth to travel before they are properly qualified, & putting them under the directions of persons, in every respect, unfit to accompany them. The young squire is often a kind of mail [*sic*] hoyden, without taste, knowledge, or manners, and the tutor a needy scholar, a *Scotsman*, or a *Swiss*, who knows no more of life than his pupil, and who, when he has put on his bag wig and sword, is one of the most awkward and ridiculous figures that can be imagined. While these grotesque characters are in a foreign country, they are the dupes and the laughing stocks of all that deal with them, or see them, and, when they return out of it, they have

---

work cited in note 12 above, Part X, I, pp. 200–201), described a complicated financial arrangement with Dalton, and added: "I have lately heard that he Dalton [intends] to publish something against the authenticity of Palmyra, and purposes to call on your lordship to support the charge. Should he do this without your lordship's knowledge, he must be strongly fortified with impudence." Robert Adam summed up Dalton to his brother John, 4 December 1756 (ERO, GD18/4826): "He is well known at Rome, where those of true taste esteem him one of the most Ignorant of Mortals. He went with Lord Charlemont to Greece, Athens, &ca., & on his return publish'd a book of the Temples &ca. he had seen there, which is so infamously stupid and ill done that it quite knock'd him in the head, & entitled him to that name of Dulton which is generally given to him. But as he had commissions from my Lord to buy up prints and Drawings for him, he had got these names by Rott & so tips You the Connoisseur with assurance and that presence of Mind that attends his Nation of Ireland."

16. Fritz Saxl and Rudolf Wittkower, *British Art and the Mediterranean*, London, 1948, p. 57.

generally picked up a sufficient number of exotic follies to be equally ridiculous at home.[17]

Lady Mary Wortley Montagu wrote of the Englishmen in Rome around 1740, during the decade when Stuart and Revett were there, as having no knowledge of the Italian language or customs, no cultural inclinations, and no interest in moving outside of their immediate circle.[18]

Though these travellers generally knew little of antique art, they were interested in collecting, either as evidence of their culture, as souvenirs, or as a financial investment.[19] As the gentlemen moved to Italy in greater and greater numbers, so did the English artists, who wished to establish connections with this group for their immediate profit and future welfare. For the most part, the artists were English painters and *ciceroni*, who did know Italian, were familar with the antiquities of Rome, had at least some knowledge of the classics, and could act as intermediaries between the English gentlemen and their Roman environment. Brettingham and Hamilton as purchasers of antique art, and Stuart and Revett as painters and possibly *ciceroni*, moved in this circle. But though the *cicerone*, or "Antiquarian" to the "English cavaliers", was sometimes disparaged as requiring an "oily supple disposition" with the assumption of "little Arts & pretensions to antient Erudition"[20] there was more to the profession, and enough of the original spirit of the Grand Tour remained so that

---

17. *GM*, XXVII, March 1758, p. 172. Also see A. C. P. Caylus to P. M. Paciaudi, 22 July 1765 (*Correspondance inédite du Comte de Caylus . . .*, ed. Nisard, Paris, 1877, II, p. 150): "Vous savez que les Anglais ne me tournent pas la tête, et qu'au contraire, ayant été trois fois chez eux, je les vois peut-être plus du côté de leurs défauts et de leur mauvais goût que de leurs bonnes qualités".

18. Lady Mary to Lady Pomfret, March 1740 (*The Complete Letters of Lady Mary Wortley Montagu*, ed. R. Halsband, Oxford, 1966, II; *1721–1751*, p. 177): ". . . Here are inundations of them [boys and governors] broke in upon us this carnival, and my apartment must be their refuge, the greater part of them having kept an inviolable fidelity to the languages their nurses taught them. Their whole business abroad (as far as I can perceive) being to buy new cloaths, in which they shine in some obscure coffee-house, where they are sure of meeting only one another. . . . I find the spirit of patriotism so strong in me every time I see them, that I look upon them as the greatest block-heads in nature; and, to say the truth, the compound of booby and *petit maître* makes up a very odd sort of animal. . . ."

19. A. S. Turberville, *Johnson's England*, London, 1933, II, pp. 16–18, describing the English craze for buying, quotes a Roman as saying: "Were our ampitheatre portable, the English would carry it off". Also see Henri Focillon, *Giovanni Battista Piranesi*, Paris, 1918, p. 60.

20. Thomas Jones, "Memoires of Thomas Jones", *Walpole Society*, XXXII, 1946–1948, pp. 74–75.

many scholars could be found among the patrons and their guides. Whatever the relationship of Stuart to this group, his interest in scholarship and his friendship with such men as Dawkins and Charlemont connected him with those English who still kept alive the original intent of the Grand Tour.

The assistance of the painter in his roles of portrait painter, history painter, and judge of other painters, seems to have been especially necessary to the English traveller. Gavin Hamilton and Thomas Jenkins (better known as a dealer in antiquities) were outstanding members of this group; Charlemont hired the painter John Parker to collect art for him in Rome;[21] and although it may be that Stuart intended as part of his Roman itinerary to perfect himself in the sciences which would later enable him to practise architecture,[22] and that Revett knew a considerable amount about the techniques of architectural drafting, these two men still were referred to as painters by Wood in his *Palmyra*.[23] Perhaps only English painters in Rome could have initiated such an expedition as Stuart's and Revett's. The painters formed a new taste based on the immediate knowledge of the taste of their patrons, with whom they acted in a partnership to which the patrons brought a love of the antique, partly through literary knowledge and partly through a tradition of collecting, and to which the painters contributed attempts at reconstituting in concrete terms the lost world of the classical age.

It was within the context of the Grand Tour that the Society of Dilettanti emerged sometime late in 1732.[24] The origins of the Society are

21. See Adolf Michaelis, *Ancient Marbles in Great Britain*, Cambridge, 1882, pp. 76–80, on Jenkins; and Michaelis, "Die Gesellschaft der Dilettanti in London", *Zeitschrift für bildende Kunst*, XIV, 1879, pp. 106–107, on other painters and their relation with the English nobility.

22. *AA*, IV, p. xxiii.   23. *Palmyra*, p. b r, note a.

24. Besides L. Cust, work cited in Chapter I, note 65, and A. Michaelis, article cited in note 21 above, see Cecil Harcourt-Smith, *The Society of Dilettanti: Its Regalia and Pictures*, London, 1932; William Richard Hamilton, *Historical Notices of the Society of Dilettanti*, London, 1855 (reviewed *Edinburgh Review*, CV, April 1857, pp. 493–517); "The Society of Dilettanti", *Chambers's Journal*, XIII, 24 March 1860, pp. 179–181; and Hans Hecht, *T. Percy, R. Wood und J. D. Michaelis*, Stuttgart, 1933, pp. 55–70. The Society of Dilettanti Letterbooks are on deposit at the British Museum, and the Minutebooks at the Royal Society of Antiquaries. I am grateful to Miss Edith Clay, who is working with this material, for helping me to gain access to it, and to the Society of Dilettanti for its kind permission to see the Minutebooks.

obscure. Founded by forty or fifty young men, all of whom had been in Italy and were peers or the sons of peers, the original members apparently had met in Rome or Venice, and, liking each other's society, decided to continue their association in England. Walpole's well-known comment on the Society: "... the nominal qualification is having been in Italy, and the real one, having been drunk: the two chiefs are Lord Middlesex and Sir Francis Dashwood, who were seldom sober the whole time they were in Italy",[25] is probably accurate. And, indeed, in its origins the members of the Society seemed no different from the majority of titled Englishmen who travelled on the Grand Tour at this time, for whom the Italians had a saying: "Inglese italianato è un diavolo incarnato."[26]

However, the Society also was a patron and promoter of the arts: in this field it moved in whatever direction enthusiasm prompted—the patronising of Italian opera, the intended founding of an Academy of the Arts, the organizing of a lottery for a bridge, the building of a permanent home for the Society, deliberations on publishing a book of poetry, and as late as 1761 the Society appointed a committee to consider the question of procuring casts of sculpture for the use of the public.[27] Vertue referred to the Society as "the Grand Clubb for promoting the arts of Drawing, Painting, etc".[28]

The leading spirit, if not the founder, of this Society was Sir Francis Dashwood,[29] and it is his character which appears to have set the tone for the first years of the Society's existence. He probably was the most widely travelled of the group, though his travels were guided less by a thirst for

25. *Horace Walpole's Correspondence*, ed. W. S. Lewis, New Haven, 1954, XVIII, Part 2, p. 211; Walpole to H. Mann, 14 April 1743. The minutes of the Society confirm Walpole's opinion: "The Committee growing a little noisy and drunk and seeming to recollect that they are not quite sure whether the Report of the Committee signed by the Chairman and Toastmaster Holdernesse may not be so intelligible to the Society as the meaning of the Committee have intended . . ." (quoted in L. Cust, work cited in Chapter I, note 65; p. 52).

26. A. Michaelis, article cited in note 21 above, p. 66.

27. See L. Cust, work cited in Chapter I, note 65; pp. 42–45.

28. Cited in William Thomas Whitley, *Artists and Their Friends in England 1700–1799*, London and Boston, 1928, I, p. 157.

29. See L. Cust, work cited in Chapter I, note 65; pp. 9–13, for biographies of Dashwood and other early members of the Society.

knowledge than for adventure. He succeeded in being expelled from the Vatican for his outrages on religion and morality, and in Russia attempted an assignation with Tsarina Anne by masquerading as Charles XII of Sweden. He continued to invent similar diversions when he founded the notorious Hell Fire Club.[30] But Dashwood was also an enthusiastic and intelligent patron of antiquity, as were other members of the Society: Lord Bessborough, who accompanied Sandwich to the Levant, was one of the earliest and most active collectors of art in England; Joseph Spence, now known for his essays on aesthetics, was one of the founding members of the Society; and the brothers Gray (Sir James, who was helpful to Stuart and Revett in Venice, and Colonel George, who published an early *Antiquities* proposal[31] and later was advisor on several architectural projects with which Stuart was connected[32]) were interested sponsors and patrons of art and antiquarian research.

It is in the Society's capacity as patron of the arts that Stuart and Revett were elected members. With their admission to the Society began the gradual change in the aims of this group which eventually made it an important instrument in formulating taste and in promoting archaeological research. After the election of the two artists their first patrons gradually were admitted. First, Rockingham was nominated on 2 February 1755. Stuart's oldest patron, he stood closest to the original character of the group, for his interests and ambitions remained diverse. On 6 April 1755 Stuart proposed for membership Dawkins, who did not live long enough to impress his character on the Society. The year after Dawkins was nominated (March 1756) he proposed Charlemont, who later headed the committee superintending and managing the *Antiquities of Ionia*, but removed himself to Ireland in 1770. Possibly owing to friction with Stuart,[33] Wood did not join the Society until 1 May 1763

30. See Edwin Beresford Chancellor, *The Lives of the Rakes*, IV: *The Hell Fire Club*, London, 1925. The best source on this club is Charles Johnstone, *Chrysal, or the Adventures of a Guinea*, London, 1760, Chapters XIX–XXX.

31. Appendix I, entry D.

32. For instance, the Society of Dilettanti clubhouse and Spencer House.

33. See pp. 32–33 below.

(nominated by Richard Phelps[34]). He may be directly responsible for the ultimate change in the character of the Society, for soon after his election funds from assessments for the club's many interests were elected to be used for a new expedition to the Levant—this time to Ionia. This expedition, the first archaeological expedition to be controlled by an organization, was based on the principles that the *Antiquities of Athens* proposals had established. The instructions demanded a thorough and systematic method of study.[35] They also established that the position of a classical scholar on the team was most important, as it had been with Stuart and Revett. The fact that Richard Chandler, a well-known classical scholar, was chosen for this position, although Revett had made a previous trip, might indicate Revett's lack of the classical education that would have enabled him to fill this post; or Chandler may have been chosen at Wood's insistence because of his laudatory comments on *Palmyra* and *Balbec*.[36] Revett took his original post, that of architectural draughtsman. William Pars as third man on the team continued the role of artist that Stuart had assumed. The resulting *Antiquities of Ionia* was the logical outcome of the *Antiquities of Athens*. Scholarly, accurate, informative, emphasizing a full presentation of visual material, the work succeeded in fulfilling in fact the intended scope and methodological thoroughness of its prototype.

The transition of the Society from its first stage of a social club with pretensions to promoting the arts to its later role as the chief patron of archaeological expeditions and publications, was echoed in the later careers of Stuart and Revett. Stuart, the older of the two men, represented the traditional classical scholarly approach to antiquity. His point of view corresponded to that of the English gentlemen whose social position required at least token participation and interest in the arts. The cultural pretensions of these men were a bond uniting them in a social

34. This Richard Phelps is doubtless the same Phelps who sponsored Mylne's trip to Sicily (see Appendix II, entries 159–164), and also may be the same Phelps who accompanied Bouverie and Dawkins to Italy (see note 44 below).
35. "Society of Dilettanti Instructions for Mr Chandler, Mr Revett, and Mr Pars", from Richard Chandler, *Travels in Asia Minor and Greece*, emendations by Revett, Oxford, 1825 (1st ed. 1817), I, p. xxi.
36. R. Chandler, *Marmor Oxoniensia*, Oxford, 1763, p. v.

group that stressed camaraderie but lacked a sense of direction and goal for its activities. Stuart's many scattered interests reflect the character of this society.[37] He was patronized as an architect, painter and connoisseur from the time that he returned to England, and his patrons were connected closely to the original group of the Society. Indeed, Stuart's prosperity may have been the result of harmony of personality with this group rather than excellence in the arts, for, except as an architect, he is not remembered for his artistic works, which, however, were praised in his own day.[38] He was over forty years old when he finally achieved success; he seems to have welcomed his new life, but his affluence and social connections allowed him to indulge himself at the expense of his work, as they doubtless played an important part in the delay in publication of the *Antiquities*. It may have been his relation to the first group of the Society, with its love of drinking and merry-making, that contributed to his own deterioration.[39] He allowed his architectural practice to be neglected, and those records of his many projects not already destroyed in his lifetime

37. Incomplete projects by Stuart are listed in BM, MS Add. 22.152. See also Chapter I, note 12. In addition to his other talents, Stuart was a sometime poet. In a request for payment, written to Mrs Elizabeth Montagu, February 1761 (*Elizabeth Montagu . . .*, ed. E. Climenson, New York, 1906, II, p. 232), he represented himself as an English hunting horse dragging Greek treasure to Mrs Montagu and addressing her in verse:

> Fairest and best! hail Montagu Minerva!
> Smile on my labours. Say that my rich freightage
> Amply deserved the Price and Pains it cost.
> So that the Muses thy companions dear,
> The Graces and the Virtues all approve
>   My bold Emprise:
> And end at once and recompense my toil.

38. Joseph Farington, *The Farington Diary*, ed. James Greig, London [1923–1928], I: 1793–1802, p. 308, 27 May 1801: "Jones told me that [Raphael] Mengs, the German painter, who was in great repute at Rome, said that He never met with but two English artists of superior genius, they were R. Wilson and Athenian Stuart".

39. Stuart's work on his return from Greece is documented in L. Lawrence, article cited in Chapter I, note 5; pp. 137–144. Stuart's personal life on his return from Europe can be summed up from several sources: his first wife was a "Grecian lady", whom he married about 1760 (according to John Nichols, *Literary Anecdotes . . .*, IX, p. 146, his first wife was his housekeeper); his second wife was the daughter of a farmer (BM, MS Add. 27.576, pp. 100–01), she was a servant previous to her marriage, and accepted Stuart after her sister had refused him. Stuart sent her to school to be educated, and married her when she was about sixteen years old. His time in later life was spent playing skittles with his cronies in the afternoon and sitting in the public house in the evening (BM, MS Add. 22.152, Memo 20 June 1808).

were lost after his death due to his unhappy choice of executor.[40]

It was Revett, a dedicated servant, and not Stuart, who continued the work they had begun together, for the *Antiquities of Ionia* in the capacity for which he was equipped, that of architectural draughtsman.[41] It is he, and not Stuart, who carried out the original intent of the *Antiquities of Athens* by supplying missing measurements for the second volume, and who co-operated with editors on succeeding volumes until his death. His position indicated the new and important role given to the architectural draughtsman in the *Antiquities of Athens* expedition; it was his measured drawings that set the standard for much of the work that followed, and made the architecture of Greece accessible to the artist, connoisseur, antiquarian and archaeologist. His architectural work, though original and advanced for its day, was small in bulk: his time seems to have been devoted to the first volume of the *Antiquities of Athens*, then to the *Antiquities of Ionia*, and finally to the second volume of the *Antiquities of Athens*. He doubtless had little initiative and probably little incentive, to assume a profession; though sociable, he was of a retiring nature.[42] He had financial difficulties dating from his travels abroad on which he apparently spent most of his patronage,[43] but his single-minded attention to his work indicates that he was a free agent in the choice of his occupation.

The expeditions to the Levant sprang from the atmosphere of the Grand Tour: from 1750 they reflected the impact of the early Stuart and Revett proposals. Thus the idea for the 1750 voyage of James Dawkins,

40. BM, MS Add. 27.576, p. 9. According to the account of an old servant: "... the person who was constituted our Agent and Guardian ... fell into loose and dissipated habits [and] ... died of maddness in a London Workhouse".

41. Revett's work on his return from Greece is documented in L. Lawrence, article cited in Chapter I, note 5; pp. 144–145. Also see Albert Edward Richardson, "Nicholas Revett", *AR*, XLIII, January–June 1918, pp. 104–106.

42. John Nichols, *Literary Anecdotes* ..., IX, p. 148, described Revett as "occasionally enlivening a small, select circle of friends with his lively conversation".

43. See L. Cust, work cited in Chapter I, note 65; pp. 97–101: *GM*, LXXIV, Part 2, September 1804, p. 860: and Appendix II, entry 139.

John Bouverie and Robert Wood[44] grew out of the knowledge by Dawkins and Bouverie of the pending Stuart-Revett expedition, which at least Dawkins helped to finance.[45] In line with the proposal of the *Antiquities*, Dawkins' voyage was to be undertaken not only for the entertainment of the three men, but also for the "advantage to the publick".[46] Accurate draughting of the monuments was considered important from the outset, for an able draughtsman and engraver, Torquilino Borra,[47] was included in the project. More specifically taken from the *Antiquities* was the emphasis on visual presentation, the idea of following the method of Desgodets, and the importance of reporting on "countries where architecture had its origin",[48] even though the eventual publications, the *Ruins of Palmyra* and the *Ruins of Balbec*, were composed of late Roman (rather than Greek) examples.

44. On this expedition, see C. A. Hutton, "The Travels of 'Palmyra' Wood in 1750–51", *Journal of Hellenic Studies*, XLVII, 1927, pp. 102–128. Original diaries and notebooks by Wood, Dawkins and Bouverie, and sketches by Borra are in the collection of the Society for the Promotion of Hellenic and Roman Studies, London. For Dawkins, see *DNB*. James Boswell, *The Life of Samuel Johnson*, ed. H. Morley, London, 1885, IV, pp. 75–76, said: "The only instance that I have known of the enjoyment of wealth was that of Jamaica Dawkins, who going to visit Palmyra, and hearing that the way was infested by robbers, hired a troop of Turkish horse to guard him." (Cited in H. Hecht, work cited in note 24 above, p. 63, note 1). For Bouverie, see *DNB*; Arthur Collins, *Peerage of England*, ed. Sir Egerton Brydges, London, 1812, V, pp. 32–33. Bouverie's and Dawkins' travelling tutor in Italy was Richard Phelps (John Nichols, *Illustrations of the Literary History of the Eighteenth Century*, London, 1817–1858, I, pp. 713–742). For Wood, see H. Hecht, work cited in note 24 above; *DNB*; and T. J. B. Spencer, "Robert Wood and the Problem of Troy", *JWCI*, XX, 1957, pp. 75–105.

45. See Chapter I, note 17, for references to Dawkins' financial aid.

46. *Palmyra*, p. a *v*.

47. According to *DNB*, on Wood's second journey to the East in 1742, he was accompanied by a Signor Borra. This man may have been the draughtsman for the Dawkins expedition. However, M. J. Craig, work cited in note 12 above, p. 55, note 6, felt that the Dawkins draughtsman was a Squire Dorra connected with Charlemont, and suggested the possibility of Wood and Charlemont having considered a joint trip. C. Harrison Townsend's suggestion that Dawkins also acted as draughtsman on the expedition ("The Royal Institute Library and Some of Its Contents", *JRIBA*, 3rd Series, XIX, 1912, p. 437) seems to be verified in contemporary accounts (see Appendix II, entries 7, 18, 38).

48. *Palmyra*, p. a *v*: "... All lovers of that art [architecture] must be sensible that the measures of the antient buildings of Rome, by Monsieur Desgodetz, have been of the greatest use: We imagined that by attempting to follow the same method in those countries where architecture had its origin, or at least arrived at the highest degree of perfection it has ever attained, we might do service."

However, the expedition was financed by the participants, Dawkins and Bouverie, and as a result was the most self-determined and individual of all the voyages of this group. In contrast to the *Antiquities*, the studies of the monuments at Palmyra and Balbec were cursory, since the amount of time spent at the sites was extremely limited,[49] and the emphasis of these books was on views and ornamental details rather than on carefully studied measurements. Also, there was one major difference between these two publications and the *Antiquities*, their literary emphasis. Both Bouverie and Wood were classical scholars, and Wood had previously travelled to the Levant:[50] these two men and Dawkins spent a winter in Rome studying classical history and geography preparatory to setting out. The library with which they stocked their ship consisted "chiefly of all the Greek historians and poets, some books of antiquities, and the best voyage writers".[51] They hoped to be able to reconstruct historical events on the exact spot where they had taken place: Wood stated in the preface to *Palmyra* that he spent two weeks with Homer in hand making a map of the plain of the Scamander.[52]

It is possible that plans were made for publication of *Palmyra* and *Balbec* from the outset of the voyage, and that Wood, a classical scholar, was included on the trip as an essential contributor to these works. Such plans could not help but compete with the work of Stuart and Revett, in spite of the fact that Wood carefully avoided Greece, leaving this country to

49. Wood dated the stay at the Palmyra between 14 and 27 March 1751, or a total of thirteen days, and gave 1 April as the date of arrival at Balbec. LeRoy, *Ruines*, 1770, p. vj, note a, and *Observations sur les edifices* . . . , Paris and Amsterdam, 1767, pp. 8–9, stated that Wood spent a total of only seventeen days in the two cities. Adam thought Wood spent fifteen days at Palmyra (Appendix II, entry 28). But the most reliable source, C. A. Hutton, work cited in note 44 above, p. 125, calculated that Wood was in Palmyra only five days. In Dawkins' diary, cited in note 44 above, he stated that the party was in Balbec on the evening of the 24th: he noted that they had finished measuring at Balbec by 29 March so that only four working days were spent here, or a total of nine working days in all (the diary is missing the period 5–22 March).

50. In May 1742 from Venice to Corfu, and from Mitylene to Scio; in February 1743 from Latakia in Syria to Damietta in Egypt: see Bernard Herbert Stern, *The Rise of Romantic Hellenism in English Literature 1732–1786*, New York, 1940, p. 30.

51. *Palmyra*, p. a v.

52. *Ibid.*, p. a r.

Dawkins' protégés.[53] Moreover, Wood's work, and not Stuart's, remained the most popular during his lifetime, and of all the early travellers to the Levant, it was Wood who proved the most attuned to the taste of his time.[54] That Wood was not elected to the Society of Dilettanti until a year after the publication of the *Antiquities*, in spite of the fact that all other persons closely connected with Stuart's expedition long since had become members,[55] must be due to personal friction. Stuart mentions in his notes to the *Antiquities*, out of context, a map of the Gulf of Zeitune which he lent Wood, and which was never returned[56]—possibly Stuart's oblique way of saying that Wood had profited from his material and ideas. Wood at some time may have contemplated a publication on Greece,[57] a project which would not allay Stuart's suspicions.

The expedition of LeRoy was of an entirely different character: LeRoy's friendship with his fellow-student at the French Academy in Rome, Charles-Louis Clérisseau, who entertained anti-academic notions and had English connections, and LeRoy's increasingly "haughty" attitude toward existing authority,[58] made him a good intermediary for the transposition of English ideas into French terms. LeRoy's voyage was both independent and official: he was financed by "le meilleur des

53. *Palmyra*, p. b r, note a. But the forthcoming *Antiquities* also may have undermined the reputation of Wood's work (see Appendix II, entry 28).

54. Adam apparently recognized this in his unpublished preface to *Spalatro* (Appendix I, entry L), when he gave Wood credit for establishing the new taste. The high esteem in which he held Wood is reflected in Adam's letter to his sister Betty, 24 August 1755 (ERO, GD18/4785): "We are at a vast loss for the want of Mr Wood whose character is one of the most perfect among the Human Race, He is of universal learning posess'd of all Languages & having travelled over all the World to the best of purposes, has fund of Storys Serious & diverting which adapts him to all Capacitys as a Learned, or as a Jovial Companion. He is intimate with all the Great people of all Nations & esteemed by those of his own I mean of England. For his Birth is Irish, His Education in part Scotch & his improvement he made in Holland, in France & Italy."

55. See pp. 27–28 above.

56. *AA*, IV, p. vii: "Messrs. Dawkins and Wood took with them the plan I made of the gulf of Zeitune. I kept no copy, and have not since seen the original."

57. According to David Lysons, *The Environs of London*, London, 1792–1796, I, p. 420, Wood was "meditating future publications relating to other parts of his tour, especially Greece, when he was called upon to serve his country in a more important station . . . "

58. See *CD*, XI, pp. 15–16, C. Natoire to Marquis de Vandières, 27 February 1754: and pp. 503–503, C. Natoire to A. F. Marigny, 30 July 1755, for opinions of LeRoy at the French Academy in Rome.

D

Pères"[59] (who was horologer to the King), while connections were established for him in the East through the French Academy in Rome,[60] and he was aided in his research and publication by the Académie des Inscriptions et Belles-Lettres[61] and the antiquarian-connoisseur, the Comte de Caylus.[62] In spite of LeRoy's claim that his voyage was within the national tradition,[63] Stuart rightly stated that the early *Antiquities* proposals were the starting-point for this project.[64] The ultimate outcome, the *Ruines . . . de la Grèce*, followed the 1748 contents proposed by Stuart, being arranged first of views and then of architectural details. Moreover, it was not until 1767, and later in 1770 in the second edition of the *Ruines*, that, defending his work, LeRoy spoke disparagingly of Desgodets.[65] But if LeRoy borrowed his arrangement from Stuart, his style was in imitation of the easy and relaxed manner of Wood, including a history of the voyage for "variety",[66] and borrowing the idea for a list of inscriptions, separate from the rest of the work, from the Palmyra publication.[67] However, LeRoy's emphasis on reduction of details, on typical proportions, and on the inclusion of only the most beautiful ornaments in his work, as well as his co-ordination of history and theory with architecture, were within the French tradition.[68]

The influence of the Stuart-Revett proposals did not stop with LeRoy. The type of publication suggested by these two men, and first realized in

59. *Ruines*, 1758, p. vj.
60. *Ibid.*
61. *Ibid.*, p. viij.
62. Appendix II, entry 78.
63. One of the reasons for undertaking the project was "le desir d'exécuter une petite partie du magnifique projet formé dans le siècle passé par notre Nation . . ." (*Ruines*, 1758, p. vj).
64. Chapter I, note 56.
65. *Ruines*, 1770, p. vj, note a; *Observations sur les édifices des anciens peuples . . .*, Amsterdam, 1767, p. 8.
66. *Ruines*, 1758, p. vij: "Afin d'éviter l'espece de monotonie que la description successive d'un trop grand nombre de Temples ou d'autres Edifices auroit pu répandre sur l'Ouvrage, j'y mêle quelques particularités de mon Voyage . . .". Compare with *Balbec*, p. 1: "If in this preliminary discourse we intermix a few observations of our own, not so necessarily connected with the subject, it is with a view to throw a little variety into a very dry entertainment."
67. LeRoy acknowledged his indebtedness to Wood in *Observations*, 1767, p. 3. See Appendix I, entry K, and Appendix II, entry 58, for the intention to model the *Ruines* after *Palmyra*.
68. See Appendix II, entry 76, and *Ruines*, 1770, p. vj, for LeRoy's comments on the difference between his work and Stuart's.

terms of folio size and a combination of scholarly and architectural contents by Wood, was continued by Robert Adam (who indicated his intention of rivalling the earlier work of Stuart and Revett[69]); Charles Cameron (who justified his *Baths of the Romans* in terms first stated in the *Antiquities*' proposals[70]); Charles-Louis Clérisseau (who attempted a continuation of Desgodets' work[71]); Giovanni Battista Piranesi (whose archaeological publications followed the type established in the 1750s[72]); by work that was later done in Southern Italy and Sicily;[73] and, finally, by the great publications of the Society of Dilettanti, which stretched into the nineteenth century.[74]

69. See Appendix II, entry 87.

70. *The Baths of the Romans Explained and Illustrated with the Restorations of Palladio Corrected and Improved*, London, 1772, p. i: "Whatever light may be produced from the laborious researches of these men [previous authors on Roman antiquities]; or whatever praise we may be inclined to allow them on account of the materials they have collected: it must be acknowledged that their pains had been better bestowed, had they, before they entered upon so comprehensive a plan as the illustration of antiquity, joined a proper knowledge of Architecture to that of books: and, instead of wresting obscure passages in antient authors to their own forced interpretations, if they had carefully compared the Works of these writers with the Ruins of the buildings they mean to describe, we should then have been furnished with proof instead of argument, and certainty in the room of doubt."

71. *Antiquités de la France*, I: *Monuments de Nîmes*, Paris, 1778. See Chapter IV, note 33.

72. For instance, *Antichita di Cora*, Rome, 1764. Also see the later *Différents vues de qvelqves sreste de trois grandes édifices qvi svbsistent encore dans le miliev de l'ancienne ville de Pesto* . . . , Rome, 1778.

73. Besides the work at Paestum (see S. Lang, "The Early Publications of the Temples at Paestum", *J WCI* XIII, 1950, pp. 48–64), there were chiefly the Sicilian publications by C. Andrea Pigonati, *Stato presente degli antichi monumenti siciliani*, [Naples], 1767; and Jean Houel, *Voyage pittoresque des isles de Sicile, de Malte et de Lipari* . . . , Paris, 1782–1787, 4v. Expeditions by such architects as Robert Mylne to Sicily, where he measured the ruins with the idea of later publishing them (see Appendix II, entries 159–164), were also undoubtedly influenced by the archaeological atmosphere first voiced in the *AA* proposals, as was a projected expedition of Wood to Sicily, mentioned by Robert to James Adam, 31 May 1755 (ERO, GD18/4774): "This poor devil [Clérisseau] has such affection for me that Though he had an offer to go with Mr Wood to Sicily to make Views of the antiquities their; which would both be honourable & profitable for him, He told me that if they woud give him all the money they were worth he woud not leave me unless I turn'd him out a Doors."

74. See Chapter I, note 30.

CHAPTER III

Reception of the Archaeological Publications

A FTER Stuart's and Revett's 1748 proposal the first publication of material taken from drawings made during a trip to the Levant was that of Richard Dalton. For our purposes the most important of his publications was the *Musaeum Graecum*, which appeared in 1752, but this work received almost no public recognition,[1] and was over-shadowed by later works in the field. Its relative obscurity was due to a number of causes: not only were the illustrations poor in quality and without architectural interest, but also the work did not have the scholarly background that Dalton's fellow-voyager Charlemont could have supplied, and the engravings alone did not provide the wealth of literary and historical detail that was to assure the popularity of the other publications.

Dalton's career in this field was brought to a close by the appearance of the first major archaeological work of the Levant, Wood's *Ruins of Palmyra*, published on 20 November 1753.[2] As an authentic pictorial record of a distant and legendary land, treated with classical scholarship, Wood's work was an immediate success in England and in France.[3] To the general public the book was connected with contemporaneous trips such as those made to Egypt by Frederik Norden and Richard Pococke

---

1. There was probably only one notice of this publication; it appeared in a French periodical (Appendix II, entry 1). For Dalton, see Chapter II, notes 14, 15. All references in this chapter designated "entry" refer to Appendix II, unless otherwise noted.

2. For the eclipse of Dalton's work, see entry 3; and *GM*, LXI, Part 1, March 1791, p. 196. For the date of publication of *Palmyra*, see entry 9. A prospectus for *Palmyra* may have been published the preceding year (see entry 6).

3. Entries 12, 14–27.

and with the excavations of Herculaneum and Pompeii.[4] Using *Palmyra* as a guide, the reader was able to move backward in time and to reconstruct a lost civilization. In addition, the book was important for the classical scholar and antiquarian: one of the first reactions to it was the publication by Jean-Jacques Barthélemy of his Palmyrene alphabet, based on an inscription uncovered by Wood and Dawkins, in 1754.[5] Barthélemy also reviewed Wood's *Palmyra*, since, as a scholar, he was interested in the historical study of the architecture of that city.[6]

Hints of the later rivalry between England and France in the field of archaeological publications also was indicated in these first reviews. The closing statement of Barthélemy's review noted that the volume was an honour to the English nation. National pride was reflected in English publications such as the *World*.[7] The French also claimed a national interest in Palmyra, and some French critics interpreted the engravings as demonstrating that Perrault had borrowed ideas from this source for the Louvre façade, though more discerning critics felt that it might have been Wood, reconstructing the façades of his ancient temples, who borrowed from Perrault.[8]

Reviewers of *Palmyra* also began commenting on one of the most important contributions of the publications—their relationship to contemporary taste. The writer for the *Adventurer* advocated the copying of the models from *Palmyra* rather than Gothic and Chinese styles, because the classical style found in Wood's work was the keystone of architecture,

---

4. Entry 16.

5. "Réflexions sur l'alphabet et sur la langue dont on se servoit autrefois à Palmyre", *Mémoires de l'Académie des Inscriptions*, XXVI, 1754. *Philosophical Transactions*, XLVIII, 1754, pp. 690–756, and *UM*, XVII, July 1755, pp. 31–32; August 1755, pp. 82–84; contain notes on Barthélemy's work. This work, too, had its audience: Barthélemy wrote Caylus, 23 October 1755 (Barthélemy, *Voyage en Italie*, Paris, 1802, p. 28): "J'avois apporté en Italie une quinzaine d'exemplaires de ma Dissertation sur les ruines de Palmyre; on m'en dépouillé par politesse."

6. Entry 20. For more information on Barthélemy's interest in Palmyra, see Paul Pedrizet, "Les dossiers de P. J. Mariette sur Ba'albek et Palmyre", *Revue des études anciennes*, III, 1901, pp. 249–250.

7. Entry 19.

8. Entry 18. However, modern architectural historians relate Perrault's façade to Balbec—but Balbec as engraved by Marot in the seventeenth century (see Hans Rose, *Spätbarock* . . . , Berlin, 1932, pp. 114–115).

and had never been surpassed.[9] The French reviewer for the *Année littéraire* also urged contemporary artists to turn to the architecture illustrated in *Palmyra*.[10] But the *Journal brittanique* reviewer was the first to take the stand which represented the academic French position toward the English archaeological publications: he called attention to the defects of a temple at Palmyra and its deviations from the traditional architectural norm.[11]

The popularity of *Palmyra* encouraged Wood to publish his second volume on Balbec, which appeared about three and a half years later.[12] Criticism of this volume indicated the advances that had been made in relating architectural taste to the archaeological material since the publication of *Palmyra*.[13] Some French and English reviewers enthusiastically considered Wood's two publications to be an antidote to the dissolution of contemporary taste and the indolence of the artist and the public: continuing the mood of reform begun with the appearance of *Palmyra*, the *Monthly Review* critic felt that the victory of the architecture of Balbec and Palmyra over Chinese and Gothic ornament was more important than a victory in the war then taking place with France.[14] However, specific praise and objections to these publications were now made in a perceptive review in the *Année littéraire*.[15] Its readers were warned that the architecture in Wood's books, though beautiful in essence, contained defects in details. Only certain plates were recommended for use as models; the Orders (Pl. 27), the column, and a peristyle temple (Pl. 1). The reviewer feared that some plates illustrating designs deviating from traditional French academic standards might be imitated. These included illustrations of pedimented windows with no visible means of support

9. Entries 15, 17.
10. Entry 18.
11. See entry 7.
12. Entry 35.
13. Entries 38–47, 49.
14. Entry 41. See entry 44 for a similar French point of view.
15. Entry 45.

(Pl. 2), irregularly coffered ceilings (Pl. 3), and small-scale architectural members placed in ornamental patterns on flat surfaces.

The reputation and popularity of Wood's two volumes continued throughout the eighteenth century. Adam wished to emulate them in his *Spalatro*,[16] and LeRoy, as we have seen, modelled his *Ruines* in part on Wood's work. Moreover, these works were well known in France; they were published in both French and English.[17] It was thus Wood's work rather than Stuart's that became tangible evidence of ancient civilization for the scholar and the artist during the formative decade of the 1750s, while the architecture of Greece remained as remote and legendary as it had been before Stuart and Revett undertook their expedition to Athens. In later decades such readers as Horace Walpole,[18] Richard Chandler,[19] and Edward Gibbon,[20] were concerned less with the problems of taste raised by these volumes and more with scholarly method and achievement. But French distrust of these publications as literal models was still felt in the nineteenth century by Quatremère de Quincy, who criticized the influence that he claimed they had had on Soufflot.[21]

In 1758, at the height of interest in popular and visually-presented archaeological research, LeRoy published his *Ruines*. It was republished in an abbreviated English edition the following year,[22] so that England and France received a first view of Greece almost simultaneously. One French journalist patriotically said that the *Ruines* was superior to everything of this type that the English previously had produced:[23] praise of the work

16. Entries 52, 79, and Appendix I, entry L.

17. *Balbec*, p. 1: "We consider ourselves as engaged in the service of the Re-publick [*sic*] of Letters, which knows, or ought to know, neither distinction of country, nor separate interests. We shall therefore continue to publish our Work, not only in English, but also in the language of a neighboring Kingdom, whose candid judgement of our first production, under the disadvantage of a hasty and negligent translation, deserves at least this acknowledgement." See also entry 50.

18. Entries 51, 54.

19. Richard Chandler, *Marmor Oxoniensia*, Oxford, 1763, p. v.

20. Entry 55.

21. Entry 56.

22. See Marcus Whiffen, "An English LeRoy: A Plagiarization of Ruines which Appeared in 1759", *AR*, CXXVI, August 1959, pp. 119–120.

23. Entry 58.

was based on the fact that LeRoy's book, besides including accurate
measurements and a historical survey, was the first of the archaeological
works consciously designed for the use of architects—it was considered
"an attempt to restore architecture to its ancient dignity".[24] But in England only the writer for the *Critical Review* mentioned the work, and
found, as had the French, that the *Ruines*, since it was concerned with true
Greek architecture, had the advantage over *Palmyra* and *Balbec* of being a
working solution of Vitruvian principles.[25] Indeed, one of the major
differences between LeRoy's work and the English publications was that
LeRoy was concerned with translating the archaeological material into
traditional architectural terms, while the English works were designed to
widen the limits of architecture: they were restricted to empirical reporting, and left interpretation to the reader.[26] In spite of his French bias, the
Critical Review writer conformed to the English tradition when he noted
that he had been informed that the *Ruines* was often incorrect, and advised
that it could be judged only in relation to the forthcoming English work
on Athens. However, to the French LeRoy's *Ruines* remained the publication on Greek architecture. Twenty years later Clérisseau still looked
on it as one of the most important works in the field.[27]

The *Antiquities of Athens* followed three publications immediately concerned with the subject of ancient architecture; all three, published in
both French and English, were popular, important guides of taste. It is
incredible that there was still enthusiasm for another book, and an ex-

24. Entry 67. See also entries 63, 64.
25. Entry 68. The *CR* probably paralleled French publications in critical content because of the
interest in French thought of its editor, Tobias Smollett.
26. *Balbec*, p. a *r*: "It shall . . . in this, as in the former volume, be our principal care to produce
things as we found them, leaving reflections and reasonings upon them to others. This last rule we
shall scrupulously observe in describing the Buildings, where all criticism on the beauties and faults
of the Architecture is left entirely to the reader." *AA*, I, Preface, pp. ii–v: "Architecture is reduced
and restrained within narrower limits than could be wished, for want of a greater number of ancient
Examples than have hitherto been published; . . . every such Example of beautiful Form or Proportion, wherever it may be found, is a valuable addition to the former Stock; and does, when published, become a material acquisition to the Art. . . . it will certainly be a study of some delight
and curiosity, to observe wherein the Grecian and Roman style of Building differ; for differ they
certainly do; and to decide, by a judicious examination, which is the best."
27. Entry 77.

pensive one, as they all were,[28] on the same subject. Moreover, the work broke with precedent by not being published in French (the first French edition did not appear until 1793), possibly because of the type of subscriber and the kind of support originally received for the publication, but also possibly because of the declining concern of the authors with the work. The interest which the *Antiquities* did raise may be explained by its long anticipation:[29] its spreading reputation, especially after it was lampooned by Hogarth;[30] Stuart's rising fame as an architect; and by national pride. If LeRoy's book was lauded by the French and ignored by the English, the reverse was true of the *Antiquities*; it may be significant that the only English journal to publish a comment on the *Ruines*, the *Critical Review*, remained silent about the *Antiquities*.

Although this book was the first English work available on the architecture of ancient Greece, reviewers were somewhat reserved. The writer for the *Monthly Review*, while justly crediting Stuart and Revett with the original idea on which LeRoy had capitalized, and lauding the careful measurements of these two men, criticized Stuart's views as stiff and in-

28. A. C. P. Caylus to P. M. Paciaudi, 18–24 February 1765 (Caylus, *Correspondance inédite . . .*, Paris, 1877, II, pp. 86–87): "Si l'on continue à mettre l'antiquité sur le grand ton et le grand prix auquel elle est montée depuis quelques années, aucun particulier ne pourra y atteindre . . . " Dalton charged 2 Guineas each for his *Musaeum Graecum* volumes; *Palmyra* and *Balbec* cost £3 10s. each; the *AA* 4 Guineas (only 2 Guineas by subscription: in the 1752 *AA* proposal (Appendix I, entry G) the estimate was £10 or £12 st.[!] for each "exemplaire"); the *Ruines* cost 54 livres by subscription, otherwise 72 livres. Adam was insistent on the work for *Spalatro* being done in Italy by cheap draughtsmen, doubtless to keep the price of his work within reason: he was able to equal Wood's price of £3 10s. Major was able to bring his *Paestum* down to 2 Guineas again, while maintaining much higher standards than Dalton.

29. Entries 83–102.

30. Entry 98. For the caricature, see *Hogarth's Graphic Works*, ed. Yale University Press: compil. R. Paulson, New Haven, 1965, pl. 230. For contemporary comments see *GM*, XXXI, May 1762, pp. 259–261, and June 1762, p. 315; and Walpole to Elizabeth Montagu, 7 November 1761 (*Horace Walpole's Correspondence*, New Haven, 1941, IX, Part 1, p. 401): "The enclosed print will divert you, especially the Baroness in the right-hand corner—so ugly, so satisfied. The Athenian head was intended for Stewart, but was so like, that Hogarth was forced to cut off the nose." Also see Henry B. Wheatley, *Hogarth's London*, London, 1909, pp. 61–63; and, for further cartoons based on Hogarth's *Catalogue of Prints and Drawings in the British Museum*, Division I: *Political and Personal Satires*, London, 1870–1954, IV, pp. 136–139. However, Stuart did not appear to have been offended by the satire, for he displayed the print prominently on a fire-screen in his house (John Thomas Smith, *Nollekens and His Times*, London, 1949 (1st ed. 1828), pp. 19–20).

differently designed.[31] A criterion of taste seemed to have been fixed before the publication of this work. Indeed, the *Antiquities* was moving
toward one specific and eventually permanent function, the purely
archaeological publication of the nineteenth century. This spirit was
caught by the writer for the *Annual Register* who described the ingenuity,
punctilious accuracy, and new light in which every monument was set.[32]
Pierre-Jean Mariette recognized this trend in writing an enthusiastic
appraisal of the *Antiquities* to his friend Giovanni Bottari,[33] for its scientific orientation caused the French group of internationally-oriented
classical scholars with antiquarian interests, numbering such men as
Mariette and Caylus, to sympathize with the English work.[34]

The legend of the *Antiquities* as the definitive treatise on architecture
in the country of its origin remained. The publication was the basis for
Stephen Riou's *The Grecian Orders of Architecture*,[35] a book which related
the *Antiquities* and the classical monuments of Greece to the architectural
works which had preceded it, such as the publications by Serlio, Palladio,
and Desgodets. In his book, Riou did not intend to depart radically from
tradition, but to expand its context.[36] Since *The Grecian Orders* was written with the authorization of Stuart, it can be assumed that the book
demonstrated the extent to which Stuart approved of Riou's interpretation of the *Antiquities*. However, as a work illustrating antiquity with
architectural examples, the *Antiquities* was considered deficient by Johann
Joachim Winckelmann, who reacted strongly against the work when it
appeared. Frustrated by the long delay in publication, and interested in
objects as visually perceived rather than in the method by which they
were reconstructed, he expected a multitude of examples of the archi-

31. Entry 104.
32. Entry 106.
33. Entry 101.
34. German periodicals were directed toward this international audience; but they reflected a
more scholarly, conservative trend: influence on architectural taste was not considered. One of
these journals even recommended Latin texts for the archaeological publications (entry 71). On the
other hand, Italian periodicals seem to have been oriented solely toward literature, and to have contained no reviews on the archaeological publications.
35. Published in London, 1768.
36. See entries 129–131 for reception of Riou's work.

tecture of ancient Greece. LeRoy's book, with its many views and its wide selection of important monuments, was a more valuable record of ancient Greece for him than the five minor buildings published in the *Antiquities*, or the large section devoted to sculpture (which he considered to be padding) and the finicky attention to details. He summed it all up: "Monstrum horrendum ingens, cui lumen ademtum."[37]

A new approach was taken by Robert Adam in his *Spalatro*: he hoped to produce a popular book in the already overcrowded field of archaeological publications by illustrating an ancient palace, which was, according to him, a more fitting model for contemporary dwellings than antique temples, the only previous examples of ancient architecture at the disposal of modern architects. He chose Diocletian's Palace, since it was the sole known remaining dwelling of antiquity with enough grandeur to be considered as a model for contemporary domestic architecture. However, most of the reviewers of *Spalatro* were not concerned with this purpose.[38] For instance, the writer for the *Gazette littéraire* appeared to be looking for a new monumental architecture in *Spalatro* rather than the specific application of the classical remains to contemporary domestic architecture.[39] On the other hand, the writer for the *Critical Review* thought Adam should have published Diocletian's Baths instead of his palace, because he considered the Baths as more elegant, and the English nobility already better housed than people in antiquity.[40]

The reception of *Spalatro* is the first indication of a deteriorating interest in the archaeological publication. Only four major reviews appeared, three of which were French. English reception was limited to the French-oriented *Critical Review*. There was no longer a question of which country led in matters of taste. The French had captured the lead and the English now were not concerned with priority in this field. With *Spalatro* the first group of archaeological publications of the Levant came to an end. Already at the time of publication Revett was setting out for

37. Entry 108. See entries 25, 53, for a similar reaction by Pierre Patte.
38. Entries 120, 123, 125.
39. Entry 123.
40. Entry 122. See also entry 128.

Ionia: the work he would commence there would not set standards of taste, though it was expected to supply examples for the taste that had already matured, but would set the standard for publications of purely archaeological research.

We are not concerned with this descendant of the *Antiquities*, but with the less directly influenced series of publications of Paestum.[41] The earliest project for publication of the Paestum material was that of the Conte Gazola, who "discovered" the Paestum temples.[42] Gazola may have been acquainted with the Stuart-Revett project, but it is certain that Soufflot, passing through Rome in 1750 on his way to Naples, where he made measured drawings of the temples at Paestum, must have heard of the first *Antiquities* proposal, which by then was about two years old. Soufflot's connection with these ruins demonstrates French interest in publishing the well-preserved Greek temples as an answer to English publications of the Eastern Mediterranean, under stimulus of growing English-French rivalry in the now interrelated fields of taste and archaeology. The French seem to have been successful in associating their nation with the ruins of Paestum, for Piranesi's posthumous *Pesto*, published in 1778,[43] had a French text, in spite of the strong nationalist leanings of the author.

As early as 1755, publications of measured drawings of Paestum, either by Gazola with the assistance of the French, or by Soufflot, seemed about to occur:[44] LeRoy's 1756 proposal announced his intention to include part of this material in his *Ruines*,[45] However, for unknown reasons publication was postponed for eight years. Gabriel-Pierre Dumont brought

41. For the complex interrelationship of these publications, see S. Lang, "The Early Publications of the Temples at Paestum", *JWCI*, XIII, 1950, pp. 48–64.

42. See entries 140–143. For Gazola's attempts to publish his material see Paolo Antonio Paoli, *Paesti quod Posidoniam etiam dixere Rudera . . .*, Rome, 1784, pp. 3–7. Paestum was previously "discovered" in the eighteenth century by, for instance, John Breval, who also published illustrations of the Temple of Agrigentum, Sicily, in his *Remarks on Several Parts of Europe*, London, 1738, and by Bishop Berkeley (see Marcus Whiffen, "Bishop Berkeley", *AR*, CXXIII, February 1958, p. 92).

43. G. B. Piranesi, *Différents vues de qvelqves restes de trois grandes édifices qvi svbsistent encore dans le miliev de l'ancienne ville de Pesto . . .*, Rome, 1778.

44. See entry 140, and S. Lang, article cited in note 41, pp. 49–53.

45. Appendix I, entry K.

out some of this material in 1764, without scholarly comment. His engravings were inaccurate; for instance, column capitals were represented as Roman Doric, and not archaic Greek. Like Dalton's earlier work, this publication was scarcely noticed by the general public.[46] The following year six views of Paestum by Antonio Jolli, published by Filippo Morghen, caused even less comment.[47] Reception was somewhat better for John Berkenhout's *Ruins of Poestum* of 1767, which contained the history, inscriptions, and architectural analysis of Paestum, though with only four engravings (by Miller),[48] but the interest was in the text rather than the illustrations.

All these earlier works are of little significance when compared to the outstanding publication of this group, Thomas Major's *Ruins of Paestum*, published in 1768.[49] This book embraced the comprehensive purpose of the works related to the Stuart-Revett proposals, that of a statement of theoretical architectural opinion, of antiquarian interests, and of literary scholarship; all presented through the medium of the archaeological publication, and including detailed and accurate engravings. As one reviewer pointed out, its ancestors were *Palmyra*, *Balbec*, the *Antiquities*, and the *Ruines*.[50] The publication not only had a large number of French subscribers (it was published simultaneously in French and English), but also it was directly related to the work of Soufflot, who assisted Major to produce this volume. Its importance to the French is indicated by the fact that the slightly later Dumont edition, published with a French translation of Berkenhout's text, was considered as a supplement to this English work,[51] and, though Major's book was published in London, only French periodicals reviewed it.

In 1769, the first volume of the *Antiquities of Ionia* appeared,[52] and

46. G. P. M. Dumont, *Suitte de plans, coupes, profils, élévations, . . . de trois temples antiques . . . dans la bourgade de Poesto qui est la ville Poestum de Pline . . .*, Paris, 1764. Only two reviewers seem to have mentioned this work (entries 147, 148). See also entry 144, where Caylus treats the work lightly.

47. Filippo Morghen, *Sei vedute delle rovine di Pesto*, 1765.

48. [John Berkenhout], *The Ruins of Poestum or Posidonia . . .*, London, 1767. See entries 149–151.

49. Thomas Major, *The Ruins of Paestum . . .*, London, 1768.

50. Entry 155.

51. Entry 156. G. P. M. Dumont, *Les ruines de Paestum . . .*, London and Paris, 1769.

52. See entries 132–138 on the reception of the *Aniquitties of Ionia*.

marked an end to two decades of introduction to the ruins of the ancient world. There would be many other archaeological publications, but no longer wonder at the legendary marvels of antiquity being revealed to the public for the first time. The publications now were of interest to the scholar, the antiquarian and the newly-born archaeologist, for whom the drawings and commentary had special meaning. Meanwhile, the public had a large repertory of publications to use as models in judging each new one, and the architect had a widening repertory of examples from which to choose.

CHAPTER IV

The Greek–Roman Quarrel

A WELL-KNOWN episode in the quarrel about the relative excellence of Greek and Roman architecture was that centering around several works by Piranesi: namely, his *Della Magnificenza ed architettura de' Romani* of 1761 and his *Parere su l'architettura*, published in 1765. To summarize part of the fundamental study of this topic:[1] in the *Della Magnificenza* Piranesi belittled Greek architecture for lack of monumentality and excessive ornamentation, or *subdivisioni*. He further claimed that not only was native Italian Etruscan art both grandiose and simple, but also that the Romans corrected the faults of the Greek art they used. The *Della Magnificenza* was criticized by Mariette in the *Gazette littéraire*,[2] where he reaffirmed the notion of Greek superiority over Roman architecture. He argued that only Greek slaves practised architecture in Rome, and that, by introducing Greek architecture (characterized by its extreme simplicity and order through rules), they removed Roman architecture from Etruscan taste. Piranesi answered this criticism in his *Parere* where he turned against simplicity and rules; he now attacked the Greeks, Vitruvius, Palladio and the *rigoristi*.[3] He defended the vigour and vitality of a constantly inventive Roman art, in which the artist was free to choose his own forms and manner of applying them.

Another phase of the quarrel was that represented by Sir William Chambers in unpublished notes composed around the time of the second (1768) edition of his *Treatise on Civil Architecture*, and in the published

1. Rudolf Wittkower, "Piranesi's 'Parere su l'architettura' ", *JWCI*, II, July 1938, pp. 147–158.
2. "Lettre de M. Mariette sur un Ouvrage de M. Piranesi concernant les Antiquités Romaines", *GL*, 4 November 1764, pp. 232–247.
3. *Parere su l'architettura*, Rome, 1765, pp. 11–12. Wolfgang Herrmann, *Laugier and Eighteenth Century French Theory*, London, 1962, p. 192, suggests that the *rigoristi* are the "fellow-travellers of Laugier". However, see Emil Kaufmann, "Piranesi, Algarotti and Lodoli; A Controversy in XVIII Century Venice", *Essays in Honor of Hans Tietze*, Paris, 1958, pp. 309–316.

introduction to the third (1791) edition of this work.[4] In contrast to Piranesi's position, Chambers was opposed not to excessive ornamentation, the use of rules, or the stripping away of form to its essentials, but to the lack of monumentality and sophistication of Greek architecture. However, Chambers' concept of "Greek" underwent a change, for in his earlier notes he emphasized, along with comments on the Parthenon and Paestum, the two monuments most closely associated with the *Antiquities*—the Tower of the Winds and the Monument of Lysicrates; by 1791 he confined himself to a reiteration of his earlier views on the monuments of Paestum. He did not consider in his criticism the concept of Greece as defined by Mariette and stated even earlier by Chambers' countryman, Allan Ramsay.[5]

There are similarities between the points of view expressed in Piranesi's *Della Magnificenza* and in Chambers' *Civil Architecture*. Both emphasize variety, are opposed to simplicity, and favour progress and development in the arts. The two men knew each other, and it has been suggested that Chambers' ideas were a development of those of Piranesi.[6] However, though Chambers recommended the *Parere*, his comments were general and brief.[7] Both men seem to have had a different Greece in mind;

4. The lecture notes are deposited at the RIBA Library; see Appendix III for excerpts. The date of 1768 is based on the extensive repetition of material from the manuscript in Chambers' 1791 edition of his *Treatise*, where he stated (p. 26) that his criticism of Greek architecture in this edition was originally intended for inclusion in the 1768 edition of this work. Dr Eileen Harris has suggested that the manuscript may have been prepared as part of a series of lectures for the Royal Academy, founded 10 December 1768: Chambers mentioned preparing notes for these lectures in a letter to Lord Charlemont, 30 January 1771 (*Manuscripts of Lord Charlemont*, work cited in Chapter II, note 12; Part X, I, p. 305).

5. Allan Ramsay, *The Investigator*, London, 1762 (2nd ed.). The Ramsay essay first appeared as "A Dialogue on Taste" in the *Investigator*, 1757, no. 332, according to Damie Stillman, "Robert Adam and Piranesi", *Essays in the History of Architecture Presented to Rudolf Wittkower* . . . , London, 1967, p. 200, n. 23.   6. James Lees-Milne, *The Age of Adam*, London, 1947, p. 45.

7. W. Chambers, *Treatise on Civil Architecture*, London, 1791, p. 19, said only: "The last of those here mentioned [i.e., Piranesi], has published a parallel, between the fairest monuments of Greece and Rome; which is recommended to the inspection and perusal, of those who have not yet seen it." The relationship of Chambers and Piranesi does not seem to have been close: Robert Adam wrote to his brother James, 4 July 1755 (ERO, GD18/4777); ". . . Chambers, who courted Piranesi's friendship with all the Assidicity of a Lover never could bring him even to do him a Sketch of any one thing . . . " For an interpretation of the *Parere* being written as an "advertisement" "to facilitate the selling of [Piranesi's] collection", see James Barry to Edmund Burke, 8 April 1769 (James Barry, *Works* . . . , London, 1809, I, pp. 160–161).

Piranesi's Greece was that of LeRoy and the French, a Greece based on traditional literary concepts of the architecture, into which the archaeological findings were absorbed: in his diatribe against "Greek" architecture Piranesi did not extend his wrath to the *Antiquities*. On the other hand, Chambers' Greece was the Greece of the *Antiquities of Athens* and of Paestum, the Greece of an ancient and barbaric race which had not achieved enough civilization to establish rules, to develop ornament, to conceive monumental architecture, or to display variety.[8]

Since Piranesi's quarrel was with the French (though he included criticism of Allan Ramsay's *Dialogue on Taste* and Ramsay asserted that his work had inspired the *Della Magnificenza*[9]), an investigation of the quarrel must take into account French attitudes toward Greece. To the French, the association with Greece traditionally meant association with an ancient civilization that had non-Italian origins and predated Roman culture. This association provided a bond, however remote, with the classical past, and made it possible for France to claim cultural equality, or even superiority, to Italy.[10] This tradition of Greece as culturally superior to Rome began to be dominant in the 1750s.[11] It had a history, reaching back to the Renaissance, in which architectural beauty presupposed a system composed of an absolute and fundamental order, founded in nature, and best known to the Greeks.[12] But ancient Greece, prior to LeRoy's *Ruines*, was available mainly through preserved literary descriptions, legends, and monuments that were Roman rather than Greek and were felt to reflect the Graeco-Roman civilization of which they were a product, rather than to represent directly that of Greece, which was considered to be hopelessly lost. Only by studying Vitruvius

8. See Appendix III, and *Treatise on Civil Architecture*, 1791, p. 21. See also S. Lang and N. Pevsner, "Apollo or Baboon", *AR*, CIV, December 1948, pp. 271–279.

9. A. Ramsay to Sir Alexander Dick, 31 January 1762 (*Curiosities of a Scots Charter Chest, 1600–1800*, ed. Mrs Atholl Forbes, Edinburgh, 1897, p. 199).

10. See, for instance, Béat Louis de Murault, *Lettres sur les Anglaises et les Francoises*, Paris, 1725, pp. 195–196.

11. John Summerson, *Architecture in Britain, 1530–1830*, London, 1963, pp. 247–248.

12. W. Herrmann, work cited in note 3 above, pp. 25–27, summarizes the growth of the French concept of architectural superiority of the Greeks in the late seventeenth and early eighteenth centuries.

E

as well as other classical authors and ancient architecture (especially Roman architecture, which had inherited the principles of Greek architecture), would this essential beauty be approached and possibly the original models be surpassed.

The different notions about the place of Graeco-Roman antiquity within the framework of modern architecture formed the basis of the quarrel of the ancients and moderns in France.[13] The concept of absolute beauty was fundamental to French architectural thinking; the quarrel centred around the question of method, that is, the difference between emphasis on contemporary practice and the preservation of tradition.[14] In the aftermath of the quarrel occurred various attempts at a synthesis of the theories about the primacy of absolute and relative beauty. Around the middle of the eighteenth century, LeRoy divided architectural principles into three classes; the first was immutable, the other two were fixed either by general custom or by special conditions.[15] Caylus stressed historical development of the orders, though adhering to the idea of general beauty and the subordination of the artist to it.[16] But the most important attempt to synthesize the two contrasting theories was made by the German, Winckelmann. Educated in a Germany still culturally dependent on France, and admittedly knowing little about ancient architecture, it was not surprising that he relied to exaggeration on the French theoretical concept of "Greek" in his architectural study, the *Anmerkungen über die Baukunst der Alten.*[17] Whether or not he seriously thought of travelling to Greece, where he could have checked his

13. See Dorothea Nyberg, *Michel de Frémin*, "*Memoires critiques d'architecture . . .*", unpublished Ph.D. dissertation, New York University, February 1962, Chapter III.

14. *Ibid.*, pp. 9–63.

15. See *Ruines*, 1758, "Discours sur la nature des principes de l'architecture civile", p. j.

16. A. C. P. Caylus, "De l'architecture ancienne" (read 7 January 1749), *Histoire de l'académie des Inscriptions*, XXIII, 1756, pp. 286–319, p. 287.

17. Published in Leipzig, 1762. In 1759, Winckelmann had published *Anmerkungen über die Baukunst der alten Tempel zu Girgenti in Sicilien*, based on the expedition to Sicily of Robert Mylne (see Appendix II, entries 159–164). An unfinished work on ancient architecture by Winckelmann is dated 1762–1768.

observations first-hand, he did refuse many offers of trips to go there.[18]

For Winckelmann, architecture was composed of both ornamental and essential parts, and, though bound to conform in general to the laws of symmetry, harmony and proportions, could depart from these laws in details. He considered that Greek architecture developed from the essentials exemplified at, for instance, Paestum, and progressed to its highest position of a combination of essentials and ornament at Athens, while it was later degraded by the Romans, who were interested only in ornament, as at Palmyra and Balbec. Such a theory was in harmony with contemporaneous French views on the synthesis of absolute and relative beauty. Winckelmann's alignment with the French was further underscored in the fact that his *Anmerkungen*, though ignored by the English, was highly praised in France,[19] and, first written in German, received what may be its only foreign translation into French.[20]

The association of the French with Greece, and the special theoretical problems arising from the ancient-modern quarrel would be reflected at the French Academy in Rome. There can be no doubt that Piranesi was fully aware of the French post-rococo emphasis on variety within essentials, and of the French theory of the primacy of Greek architecture. It is precisely these views which he chose to criticize in his first theoretical publication, the *Della Magnificenza*. The "Greek" *subdivisioni* which he criticized may be interpreted as the ornament and variation which figured in contemporaneous French practice.[21] The *Della Magnificenza*, then,

18. Eliza Marian Butler, *The Tyranny of Greece over Germany*, Boston, 1958 (1st ed. 1935), pp. 34–35, lists six different opportunities Winckelmann had to visit Greece, all expenses paid: one of the most lavish of the offers was made in 1762 by James Adam. Bernard Herbert Stern, *The Rise of Romantic Hellenism in English Literature 1732–1786*, Menasha, Wisc., 1940, p. 82, notes seven offers between 1758 and 1767.

19. For instance, *BSBA*, XVIII, Part 1, July-September 1762, pp. 235–236. B. H. Stern, work cited in note 18 above, p. 85, does not think that Winckelmann was an important influence in England until after 1768, though Fuseli translated his works into English in 1765.

20. *Remarques sur l'architecture des Anciens*, Paris, 1783. However, Winckelmann's extreme idealism caused his theories to be incompatible with the more moderate French approach (see Jean Monval, *Soufflot, sa vie—Son oeuvre—Son esthétique (1713–1780)*, Paris, 1918, p. 501, on French opinions of Winckelmann).

21. For contemporary comments on French architectural use of detail and ornament, see W. Herrmann, work cited in note 3 above, pp. 221–234.

might indicate a reaction against the traditional and official attitude of the French Academy in Rome (against which the two Frenchmen connected with the architectural publications, Clérisseau and LeRoy, rebelled[22]). On the other hand, more advanced French thought was represented by Mariette and Laugier: now Greek architecture was simple and severe, the essential and not the variable parts of architecture were emphasized. The *Parere* of 1765 recognized these elements in French thought, and struck out against the rules and restrictions that the new method would impose.

But the Greek-Roman quarrel had a Northern background, and was connected only indirectly with Italy. Its roots lay in the older ancient-modern quarrel, which was only partially centred in the French Academy of Architecture. Within the Académie Française, and connected with the literary ancient-modern quarrel, a third point of view had developed, an extension of that of the "ancients" of the Academy of Architecture; it was a viewpoint in which the key issue was the return to original sources.[23] The concept of direct contact with the sources was first fully applied to architecture by Antoine Desgodets in 1682 in his *Edifices antiques de Rome*.[24] Desgodets' work challenged tradition by opening the way for direct consultation of the monuments without the intermediary of authoritative interpretations, such as those of Vitruvius, Serlio, Palladio or Vignola. His method was the acknowledged starting-point for the early archaeological publications connected with the *Antiquities*. Though springing from academic premises, the *Edifices* could be related to neither the rationalist and empirical approach of, for instance, Claude Perrault, since its purpose was to seek universal truths, nor to the "ancients'" point of view of François Blondel, since it by-passed the traditional authorities on which

22. See Chapter II, note 58.

23. Basic bibliography on the quarrel is: Hubert Gillot, *La querelle des anciens et des modernes en France*, Paris, 1914; and Ange Hippolyte Rigault, *Histoire de la querelle des anciens et des modernes*, Paris, 1856. However, see Richard Foster Jones, "The Background of the *Battle of the Books*", *Washington University Studies: Humanistic Series*, VII, no. 2, April 1920, pp. 99–162; and idem., *Ancients and Moderns: A Study of the Rise of the Scientific Movement in Seventeenth-Century England*, St Louis, 1961 (2nd rev. ed.), for the English background developed by Jones as distinct from the French quarrel and connected with the rise of the New Science and the Royal Society.

24. See W. Herrmann, "Antoine Desgodets and the Académie Royale de l'Architecture", *AB*, XL, March 1958, esp. pp. 43–44.

the "ancients" based their stand. Indeed, by carrying to extremes the point of view of the "ancient" and "modern" camps, the *Edifices* was in contradiction to both these branches of traditional French theory: direct contact with the sources resulted in new evaluations of the original material.

During his lifetime Desgodets' publication was not well received by the French Academy of Architecture.[25] Indeed, his work was seldom referred to by the Academy after its reappraisal following the death of François Blondel: around 1700 French students applied Desgodets' methods to Roman sites;[26] after his death in 1728 the *Edifices* was not mentioned until 16 April 1742, and 14 June 1745;[27] and the greatest interest in this work was shown by the Academy on 22 August 1746 (possibly reflecting an archaeological spirit that was developing in Rome), when a series of monuments published by Desgodets were analysed.[28] Although the work later was referred to several times in passing,[29] interest in the *Edifices* waned again and was revived only momentarily on 1 March 1779,[30] when the Academy considered the publication of the new edition.

The proposals of the *Antiquities of Athens* were the first formal statement of the recognition of the importance of Desgodets' work within the archaeological movement. The similarity of Desgodets' and English interest in archaeology was recognized again, as we have seen, by Wood and Dawkins. For the mid-eighteenth century his work was considered as a starting-point that could be improved: by 1756 Robert Adam was think-

25. *Ibid.*, pp. 24–27.

26. For Oppenord's project to verify Desgodets, see *CD*, II, pp. 239–240, M. de LaTeulière to A. Villacerf, 26 June 1696; pp. 246–247, A. Villacerf to M. de LaTeulière, 16 July 1696. For later measurements on the model of Desgodets by P. L. Moreau-Desproux, C. de Wailly and M. J. Peyre, of the Baths of Diocletian, see *CD*, XIII, p. 428, Comte d'Angiviller to J. M. Vien, 25 April 1779; and J. J. Barthélemy, *Voyage en Italie* . . . , ed. A. Sérieys, Paris, an X (1801), pp. 206–209, Barthélemy to A. C. P. Caylus, 25 January 1752; p. 204, Barthélemy to Caylus, 19 January 1757.

27. *PV*, V, pp. 316–317; VI, p. 27.

28. *Ibid.*, VI, pp. 54–55.

29. *Ibid.*, VI, p. 98, 1 April 1748; p. 146, 11 August 1750, 17 August 1750; p. 148, 7 September 1750; VII, p. 146, 30 May 1763.

30. *Ibid.*, VIII, pp. 369 ff.

ing of a corrected edition of the *Edifices*;[31] and in the 1760s the Comte de Caylus considered buying and publishing all the material on measurements of antique monuments in the French Midi, originally commissioned by Colbert as a complement to the studies of Desgodets.[32] Later this project was partially carried out by Clérisseau.[33] However, the work did not win universal approval. Not only did LeRoy speak out, though belatedly, against Desgodets,[34] but the French Academy by its silence during these years indicated its aloofness. The English not of the new archaeological persuasion were less reticent. Berkenhout, in his Paestum volume of 1767, was said to have omitted measurements "because he is of the opinion that minute accuracy in measuring the buildings of the ancients tends very little to the improvement of architecture in general".[35] By the 1770s Desgodets' *Edifices* began to be fashionable: reprints appeared from 1771. It is significant that the first eighteenth-century edition was in English, and not in French.[36] The French reissue of the original edition did not appear until 1779. From 1790 Desgodets' popularity was at its peak, with five editions before 1850.[37] Again, the Academy dimly mirrored this trend, by referring to the 1779 reprint twice in 1792.[38]

31. John Fleming, "The Journey to Spalatro" (from "A Robert Adam Miscellany"), *AR*, CXXIII, February 1958, p. 103; and *idem, Robert Adam and His Circle*, London, 1963, p. 51. A letter from Piranesi to Robert Mylne, 22[?] November 1760, in the RIBA Library (excerpted by Christopher Gotch, "The Missing Years of Robert Mylne", *AR*, CX, September 1951, p. 182) indicates that Piranesi also was engaged in criticism of Desgodets.

32. The French complement to the *Edifices* had been commissioned by Colbert from Nicholas Mignard of Avignon. See A. C. P. Caylus, *Correspondance inédite* . . ., Paris, 1877, I, p. 310, Caylus to P. M. Paciaudi, 16 May 1763; p. 342, Caylus to Paciaudi, 15 April 1763.

33. Charles-Louis Clérisseau, *Antiquités de France*, I: *Monuments de Nîmes*, Paris, 1778, p. vji: "Desgodets à qui nous devons une description assez fidèle des Antiquités de Rome, avoit aussi pris les mesures & fait les dessins de celles de Nismes: malheureusement ils sont égarés; il seroit à souhaiter qu'on les retrouvât, on pouvroit les faire servir à vérifier ceux que je présente au Public."

34. Chapter II, note 65.

35. *MR*, XXXVII, November 1767, p. 340.

36. Ed. George Marshall, London, 1771–1795 (French and English text).

37. The editions were: ed. Piroli, Rome, 1794 (including the work of other architects); ed. Charles Moreau, Paris, 1800 (supplement); ed. Fea, Rome, 1822 (Italian translation and revision); ed. Valadier-Canina, Rome, 1842–1843 (published in Italian and French, additions and corrections); ed. Charles Taylor, London, 1848 (English translation).

38. *PV*, IX, pp. 327–328, 9 July 1792; p. 329, 23 July 1792.

Although the English archaeologists used Desgodets' work as justification for the archaeological publications, the *Edifices* was not adopted without transformation. The English emphasis on measurements and accuracy went beyond that of the French model, and may have had its source in the philosophical and scientific background in England, which was the result of a historical conflict between the New Science (reflected by the Royal Society) and traditional learning, and was distinct from the French literary and aesthetic manifestations of the quarrel centring around established academies.[39] The encouragement by the Royal Society of the early voyages and scientific pursuits, and its endorsement of the method of direct observation, were partially responsible for the later archaeological expeditions.[40] Against this background Desgodets' work may have represented a formula for the extension of the English scientific spirit into the field of architecture.

Interest in the collection of data, empirical observation, precise scholarship, and even the sense of adventure of the later archaeologists and their patrons may reflect attitudes connected with the atmosphere of the Royal Society. Moreover, the anti-traditional views of the patrons of the publications paralleled the questioning spirit of the seventeenth-century "moderns". These views are illustrated by the political interests of these men. Rockingham was emphatically and unswervingly connected with the Whig Party;[41] Dawkins at one point was so closely allied with the Jacobites that he was exiled from England, though he was later recalled and served as a member of Parliament before his early death;[42] Bouverie was also a Jacobite; while others connected with the publications tended to dabble in politics, though their political achievements are either remembered as failures (Dashwood brought about the downfall of his own

39. See works by Richard Foster Jones, cited in note 23 above.

40. See Ray William Frantz, *The English Traveller and the Movement of Ideas 1660–1732*, Lincoln, Neb., 1934, Chapter I: "The Traveller and the Royal Society", pp. 15–29.

41. Rockingham held regular political-artistic meetings at Stuart's house until his death (*AA*, IV, p. xxiv).

42. *DNB*. Charles Cameron (who published *The Baths of the Romans Explained* . . . , London, 1772) was also a Jacobite.

party[43]), or as scandals (the Sandwich-Wilkes affair brought the atmosphere of the Hell Fire Club into Parliament). Of the more staid politicians of this group, Adam was a Tory, and was elected a member of Parliament, but his politics were probably part of a calculated effort to advance himself; he was never accepted fully by the Tory group, and did have connections with members of the less conservative Society of Dilettanti, for whom he did some building.[44] Wood seems to have been the only member of this group who had a successful political career,[45] though, in spite of the influence of his books, he was not concerned with architecture as a patron or as an artist.

If anything may be concluded from this array of political commitments, it is that the politics of the members of this group were highly individual, and that many of these men were on the fringe of or outside the mainstream of contemporary political action. Their views also alienated them from normal academic outlets for their interests: the fact that the Society of Dilettanti had been rebuffed in its desire to control the founding of the Royal Academy may be the reason that Stuart, a member of the Society, showed his disdain for official control of art by exhibiting the work of an absent friend with that of the rejected artists instead of in the regular Academy exhibitions.[46] The English archaeological publications connected with this group paralleled the independence from authority of the men connected with these publications by stressing the importance of individual taste.[47]

Parenthetically, Piranesi was closely allied to those English who were

43. The excise tax on cider, instituted by Dashwood, is generally considered responsible for the downfall of the Bute ministry.
44. Society of Dilettanti patrons of Adam were Bubb-Doddington and Dashwood.
45. For Wood's political career, see *DNB*, and T. Spencer, work cited in Chapter II, note 44, pp. 75–82.
46. John Thomas Smith, *Nollekens and His Times*, London, 1949, (1st ed. 1828), pp. 10–11.
47. For a political interpretation equating "Greek" with Tory and "Gothic" with Whig political Parties, see Samuel Kliger, "Whig Aesthetics: A Phase of Eighteenth-century Taste", *ELH, A Journal of English Literary History*, XVI, June 1949, pp. 135–150; "The 'Goths' in England; An Introduction to the Gothic Vogue in Eighteenth Century Aesthetic Discussion", *Modern Philology*, XLIII, November 1945, pp. 107–117; and *The Goths in England: A Study in Seventeenth and Eighteenth Century Thought*, Cambridge, Mass., 1952.

proposing freedom in architectural thinking and a new outlook that was in part a reaction to traditional French authority in the field of the arts. But the English were developing and enlarging viewpoints that were originally French, while Piranesi was opposed to the French tradition. It is interesting that one of his early publications (1756), the *Antichità Romane*, was to have been dedicated not only to an Englishman, but to one of the original archaeological voyagers and patrons of the *Antiquities*, Lord Charlemont.[48] The story of that dedication may be an indication of the hopes and disappointments that Piranesi must have had concerning English support for his too-radical views.[49]

Interest in archaeology had also developed in France, related to the English archaeological movement: it was associated with a group of internationally-oriented antiquarians, who were ridiculed by the fashionable encyclopaedists and isolated from prevailing currents of art by inclination and the dictates of fashion.[50] There were, however, members of this group who saw a wider role for antiquarianism than that ordained for it by contemporary taste: chief among these was the Comte de Caylus. His dual role as amateur archaeologist and patron of the arts made it possible for him to influence French taste.[51] By a return in subject and form to antique models, Caylus hoped to eliminate the *petite manière* from French art. It was to be expected that he would be opposed to Winckelmann's work, which was concerned primarily with the idea

48. Graham B. Tubbs, "Piranesi and Lord Charlemont", *JRIBA*, XXXVII, November–December 1929, pp. 54–56; and *Manuscripts and Correspondence of Lord Charlemont*, work cited in Chapter II, note 12, IX, Part 1, pp. 231–248.

49. For another episode in the deterioration of Piranesi's relations with the English, Robert Adam to Mrs Adam, 19 October 1756 (ERO, GD18/4821): "Jamie wishes to know of the Dedication, But realy I fancy he may dispair of it as I do, for that Piranesi is a most Changeable interested Madman, whom there is no depending on. And I beleive Jealousy may now prevent his doing what may be to my honour or advantage for as he sees I am doing things that interfere with his Province, viz making drawings of the Antique Baths &ca here, to much better purpose than he is capable of He suspects I may publish them & so hurt his fate of these things, which no doubt I intend time & place convenient to do, And so keep him entirely ignorant of what I am about & what my intentions are, which help to augment his Suspicions."

50. See Jean Seznec, *Essais sur Diderot et l'Antiquité*, Oxford, 1957, Chapter V: "Le singe antiquaire", pp. 79–96.

51. See Samuel Rocheblave, *Essai sur le Comte de Caylus: l'homme, l'artiste, l'antiquaire*, Paris, 1889, Part 2, Chapter III: "Caylus et l'antiquité.—Essai d'une réforme", pp. 199–230.

behind the work of art,[52] and would be enthusiastically interested in the new archaeological publications, considering, as we have seen, a continuation of Desgodets' work,[53] and assisting with the publication of LeRoy's *Ruines*.[54] How closely the English archaeological and the French antiquarian movements were interrelated cannot be determined now, but it is certain that there were connections between them. Caylus' circle included not only Italians and French antiquarians but also English scholars. Edward Gibbon, for instance, saw a great deal of the antiquarians during the influential 1750s.[55] Wood also, as a scholar, must have had contact with this group through such men as Paciaudi in Italy, who knew Caylus and worked with him. And at this time the Stuart-Revett project was known to these men.[56]

Another aspect of the ancient-modern quarrel was suggested in the original proposal for the *Antiquities*, which continued an ancient tradition of visiting the original site of an historical event.[57] Doubtless Wood's book followed this tradition. His concept of the relationship of architecture to its location and historical period was based on the assumption that ancient architecture could not be understood through engravings and descriptions alone: not only the ancient literature should be studied, but also the ancient monuments must be seen in order to comprehend the past. A literal rendering of the monuments, without attention to the rules imposed by tradition, was essential to a recreation of as much of their physical reality as possible. It has been suggested that Wood's approach was a result of the late seventeenth-century spirit of the French literary

52. A. C. P. Caylus to P. M. Paciaudi, 23 January 1764 (Caylus, *Correspondance inédite* . . ., Paris, 1877, I, p. 410): Soyez en sûr, d'autant que l'auteur [Winckelmann] est léger, et qu'il me fait dire ce que je n'ai pas dit. Je suis content de lui par rapport à Herculaneum, mais je continue à ne pas l'être de la façon dont il traite des arts, et je soutiens, entre nous deux au moins, qu'il s'en échauffe, mais ne les entend pas véritablement"; and, Caylus to Paciaudi, 26 February 1764 (*ibid.*, p. 423): "Le faux enthousiasme de l'auteur [Winckelmann] sur les arts est presque impossible à traduire . . ."
53. See note 32 above.
54. Appendix II, entry 78.
55. See Georges A. Bonnard, "Gibbon's *Essai sur l'Étude de la Littérature* as Judged by Contemporary Reviewers and by Gibbon Himself", *English Studies*, XXXII, August 1951, pp. 145–153.
56. See Appendix II, entry 85.
57. See Appendix I, entry C.

ancient-modern quarrel:[58] it is similar to the "ancients'" premise of a widened cultural horizon and a return directly to classical literary sources, such as Homer. Indeed, Wood felt it necessary to go to the land of Homer as well as to the original text.[59] The "ancient" side of the quarrel implied an interrelationship between literature and art, not in the traditional academic sense of both mediums following similar rules, but in the broader sense of a common goal, the re-creation of the distant past. The spectator was given a role as contributor to the work of art: he was an arbiter and judge of its merits, and through his ability to empathize the work of art could be understood. The implications of Wood's approach seem to look forward beyond the *Antiquities*, and even beyond the other archaeological publications, to nineteenth-century romanticism, with its interest in mood evoked by the specific factors of time and place.[60]

In the context of the ancient-modern quarrel, Chambers' defence of traditional approaches to architecture was not that of the "ancients", but of the "moderns", with their emphasis on the rationally understandable, on the accumulation of experience, and on the assumed upward progress of civilization. It was from this point of view that Chambers attacked the newly-discovered Greek architecture; it was a barbarian art which needed to be refined by succeeding generations. For Chambers the archaeological discoveries were separated from the main body of historical architecture because of their deviations from the established norm, their lack of monumentality, and their undeveloped character.

The new archaeological architecture which Chambers publicly attacked in the 1791 edition of his *Treatise* was defended in the third volume of the *Antiquities of Athens*, published in 1794. In specific answer

58. Hans Hecht, work cited in Chapter II, note 24; pp. 33 ff.
59. For Wood's interest in Homer, see T. Spencer, article cited in Chapter II, note 44.
60. H. Hecht, work cited in Chapter II, note 24; pp. 69–70, has suggested Wood's connection with pre-romantic trends. See also Stern, work cited in note 18 above, Chapter III: "Romantic Hellenism in the Literature of Travel to the East", pp. 38–77, for further connections of pre-romanticism with travels to the Levant. Robert Adam expressed this trend to his brother James, 24 July 1756 (ERO, GD18/4811): "To view the Temple of Athens of Thebes of Sparta; The field of Marathon & Straits of Thermophyle & though the Thought is altogether imaginary yet it is pleasing to be where harangued Demosthenes, where fought Epaminodos & where Pericles counciled . . ."

to Chambers' stand of 1791, Willey Reveley stated:

> The awful dignity and grandeur of this kind of temple [GreekDoric], arising from the perfect agreement of all of its various parts, strikes the beholder with a sensation, which he may look for in vain in buildings of any other description. . . . There is a certain appearance of eternal duration in this species of edifice, that gives a solemn and majestic feeling, while every part is perceived to contribute its share to this character of durability. . . .
>
> The Grecian Doric is by many indiscriminately censured for clumsiness. But those who are so ready to condemn it should first recollect, that it was applied only where the greatest dignity and strength were required. It happens in this, as well as in every other part of ornamental architecture, that the judicious application makes all the difference between the censure or praise it deserves. . . . Let those who prefer the later Doric indiscriminately, and entirely reject the Grecian, try whether they can, with their slender order, produce the chaste and solid grandeur of the Parthenon, or the still more masculine character of the great temple of Pesto. . . .[61]

and in this statement he summed up the architectural components of the Sublime.

The concept of the Sublime must be seen as rooted in the subjective, emotional side of the ancient-modern quarrel.[62] It can be related to the publications as early as 1756, when the poet Thomas Gray sensed that the elemental quality of the *Antiquities* was incompatible with polished culture by objecting to the "fine Lady" part of the work, that is, the courting of the subscriptions of elegant society.[63] Two years later, in 1758, Edmund Burke elaborated on this concept in his *Philosophical*

61. *AA*, III, Preface pp. xiv–xv.

62. For the development of the concept of the Sublime, see Samuel H. Monk, *The Sublime: A Study of Critical Theories in XVIII-Century England*, Ann Arbor, Mich., 1960 (1st ed. 1935); Eileen Harris, "Burke and Chambers on the Sublime and Beautiful", *Essays in the History of Architecture Presented to Rudolf Wittkower* . . . , London, 1967, pp. 207–213; and Dora Wiebenson, " 'Architecture terrible' and the 'jardin anglo-chinois' ", *JSAH*, XXVII, May 1968, pp. 136–139.

63. Appendix II, entry 86.

Enquiry into . . . the Sublime.[64] However, the small, elegant buildings, with diversified ornament, of the first volume of the *Antiquities* seem to correspond not to the Sublime, but to Burke's description of the Beautiful.[65] There may be a possibility that the final change in format of the *Antiquities* was related in part to the influence of Burke's definition of beauty (the *Enquiry* appeared three years after the last proposals and four years before the publication of the first volume of the *Antiquities*), and that Chambers' unpublished attack of the late 1760s,[66] stressing the smallness of the *Antiquities'* monuments, was also an attack on the new idea of the separation of monumentality from beauty. The Sublime was not connected directly with the archaeological publications until 1794 when Reveley defended the strength, durability, massiveness and solidity that were characteristics of the monuments of the second and third volumes of the *Antiquities* and of Burke's definition of the Sublime (for which, Burke, some thirty years before, could only offer the example of Stonehenge[67]).

One last series of transformations of the archaeological material was made by Uvedale Price.[68] He also interpreted the Greek Doric columns of Paestum as Sublime.[69] But he opposed the architecture of Paestum to Athenian architecture, which he placed in the category of the Beautiful.[70] And finally, as examples of the Picturesque, he chose the two most famous and controversial monuments of the first volume of the *Antiquities*, the Monument of Lysicrates and the Tower of the Winds.[71]

64. Edmund Burke, *A Philosophical Enquiry into the Origin of Our Ideas of the Sublime and Beautiful*, London and New York, 1958 (1st ed. 1758).

65. *Ibid.*, pp. 113–117.

66. See note 4 above, and Appendix III.

67. Work cited in note 64 above, p. 77.

68. Uvedale Price, "On Architecture and Buildings", published in *On the Picturesque . . . and Much Original Matter*, London, 1842.

69. *Ibid.*, p. 431.

70. *Ibid.*, p. 360.

71. *Ibid.*, p. 396.

CHAPTER V

Archaeology and Architecture

No discussion of the eighteenth-century archaeological publications would be complete without some consideration of their impact on architecture. The range of influence will be briefly suggested in the following account.

The first example of the adaptation to architecture of material from the archaeological publications of the Levant may have been the 1753 project for the Society of Dilettanti's clubhouse in Cavendish Square, based on reconstructions by Stuart and Revett of the Temple of Pola (Pls. 5, 6).[1] This design, with which Colonel George Gray was connected,[2] included what would become a common Neo-classical motif, the Greek Revival temple front. Although it had been pointed out that this type of temple façade was an innovation,[3] it also represented a development from the earlier long Palladian front, with a pedimented centre, made popular by Richard Boyle, Lord Burlington, and his circle.

The Burlington circle is connected also with the introduction of classical forms in gardens, which, through historical and literary associations, were intended to evoke thoughts of the ancient world. The first indication of

1. See John Summerson, "The Society's House: An Architectural Study", *Royal Society of Arts Journal*, CII, 15 October 1954, pp. 920–933. The Society of Dilettanti Minutebooks contain entries on the Clubhouse for 7 March 1742, 6 May 1750, 3 May 1752, 6 May 1753 (the first mention of the Temple of Pola as the model for the building), 2 March 1755, 1 May 1757. Records of payment for digging at the Temple of Pola (from W. R. Hamilton MS notes, mentioned in *Antiquities of Ionia*, V, 1915, pp. 1–2) may indicate that the Society had the clubhouse in mind at the time of Stuart and Revett's Pola expedition. In a Committee Report, not included in the Minutes (reproduced in William Hamilton, *Historical Notices of the Society of Dilettanti*, London, 1855, pp. 19–20), the possibility of building a Temple of Pola as a public monument, dissociated from the Clubhouse project, was discussed.

2. On the committee for the clubhouse design, see Lionel Cust, *History of the Society of Dilettanti*, London, 1898, p. 47.

3. J. Summerson, work cited in note 1 above, pp. 926–927.

an adaptation of the newly-discovered monuments of Greece to gardens may have been in 1752, when the Monument of Lysicrates was recommended as a garden structure.[4] Material from the publications probably was introduced first in a canvas backdrop of a view of Palmyra, erected in the Vauxhall Gardens in 1754,[5] less than a year after the publication of Wood's book on the ruins of this ancient city. The first architectural use of archaeological material is claimed to be Stuart's Greek Doric temple (1758) at Hagley Park, thought to have been adapted from the Hephaesteion.[6] Later garden structures were modelled after the smaller and more unusual monuments of the Levant publications. Though opposed to the influence of the publications, even Chambers designed a monument similar to the small temple from Wood's *Balbec*, at Kew Gardens in 1761.[7] But the Lysicrates Monument and the Tower of the Winds (Pls. 7–10) were the most popular monuments from the publications to be adapted to contemporary architecture. Among early modifications of these two examples are garden structures at Shugborough (Pls. 11, 12), where Stuart also erected an Arch of Hadrian and a Shepherd's Monument, here attributed to him on the basis of its similarity to his sketch of an unfinished antique column (Pls. 13, 14).[8] Probably unconnected with Chambers, a version of the Monument of Lysicrates was built at Kew

4. Richard Dalton, *Musaeum Graecum*, London, 1752, pp. 21–23: "The Temple of Hercules (vulgarly call'd *Demosthenes' Lantern*, because it is probable that it was built by him) is a very singular Piece of Architecture.... Upon the whole, I think it is agreeably singular; and that it would make a very proper Building for the Mount in your Park."

5. Elizabeth Montagu wrote to her husband, 9 July 1754 (*Elizabeth Montagu ...*, ed. E. Climenson, New York, 1906, II, p. 52), that the ruins of Palmyra were "painted in the manner of scenes so as to deceive the eye and appear buildings" at the Vauxhall Gardens. There is material on this Palmyra backdrop in Volume I of the *Vauxhall Scrapbooks*, on deposit at the Bodleian Library.

6. Lesley Lawrence, "Stuart and Revett", *JWCI*, II, 1938, p. 138. John Harris has suggested that a portico designed by Revett for his brother (mentioned in a letter to Revett from his brother in the Bodleian Library, Gough Misc. Ant. fol. 4, no. 174, dated 27 June 1757) may be an earlier example.

7. Destroyed in 1916. Published in "Sir William Chambers and Kew", *Country Life*, LXVII, 31 May 1930, pp. 792–794. Chambers described the temple in his *Plans ... of the Gardens and Buildings at Kew in Surrey*, London, 1763, p. 3. A similar garden structure was built at Stourhead, ca. 1763, by Henry Flitcroft (see Kenneth Woodbridge, "Henry Hoare's Paradise", *AB*, XLVII, March 1965, p. 95 and plates 32, 34).

8. For Shugborough, see Christopher Hussey, "A Classical Landscape Park", *Country Life*, CXV, 15 April 1954, pp. 1126–1129; 22 April 1954, pp. 1220–1223.

Gardens some time between 1763 and 1787.[9]

The French seemed to have had little or no interest in these monuments, a rare exception being a pump house designed after the Tower of the Winds, with a finial similar to that of the Lysicrates Monument, built at Plessis-Chamant in the last decades of the eighteenth century (Pl. 15).[10] After 1770 the Monument to Lysicrates was adapted to funeral and memorial structures. The first of this type was probably Joseph Nollekens' 1789 monument to William Weddell (a member of the Society of Dilettanti) at Ripon Minster (Pl. 16). A continuation of this development in the 1810s and 1820s has been documented.[11] Several pulpits also were designed after the Monument to Lysicrates; the outstanding example is at Greenwich Chapel, by James Stuart and William Newton (Pl. 17).[12]

Adaptations of the Tower of the Winds and the Monument to Lysicrates were made also on the tower stages of monumental, generally ecclesiastical, structures. This use was foreshadowed in James Wyatt's design of a modification of the Tower of the Winds for the Radcliffe Observatory tower at Oxford, commissioned as early as 1773 (Pl. 18). But the popular application of these two antique structures as stages of church towers did not begin until 1812 when James Elmes introduced a version of the Monument of Lysicrates on the tower of his St John's Chapel at Chichester, Sussex (Pl. 19). Further modifications of this monument followed in the next ten years (Pls. 20–22): a late example (1834) once existed at the Greenwich Railway Station in Deptford.[13]

9. *Country Life*, CXXVIII, 28 July 1960, p. 199, letter from John Harris to editor. Illustrated in George Louis LeRouge, *Les jardins anglo-chinois* . . . , Paris, 1770–1778, Cahier II, Plate III.

10. Also, a "lanterne de Diogène", by Jacques-Guillaume Legrand, was once in the park at Saint-Cloud, according to Michel Gallet, *Demeures parisiennes: l'époque de Louis XVI*, Paris ,1964, p. 189.

11. Hugh Honour, "Adaptations from Athens", *Country Life*, CXXIII, 22 May 1958, pp. 1120–1121. I am indebted to Mr Nicholas Cooper for reference to this article.

12. See Lesley Lewis, "The Architects of the Chapel at Greenwich Hospital", *AB*, XXIX, pp. 260–267.

13. Nikolaus Pevsner, *London, Except for the Cities of London and Westminster*, London, 1952, p. 108. Other examples are: G. S. Repton, St Philip's Chapel, Regent St., London, 1819–1820; John Foster, St George, Liverpool, 1819–1825; Robert Smirke, St George, Brandon Hill, Bristol, 1823; Robert Smirke, St Mary, Wyndham Place, Marylebone, London, 1823–1824; John Soane, St Peter's Walworth, Southwark, 1823–1825; Robert Smirke, St Anne, Wandsworth, 1824; W. and H. W. Inwood, St Peter's Chapel, Regent Square, St Pancras, 1824–1826.

A possible combination of the Tower of the Winds and the Monument of Lysicrates was initiated by William and Henry Inwood on the tower of St Pancras Church, Marylebone, 1818–1820 (Pl. 23): the polygonal stages of this tower are similar in form to the Tower of the Winds, but the free-standing columns are related, as surely was the ornamental finial from the top stage, to the Lysicrates Monument. This tower type was adapted almost without modification within several years (Pls. 24–26) to other churches.[14]

Although archaeologically-inspired garden and memorial structures are related to the work of the Burlington circle, representations of antique monuments used on monumental architecture of the 1810s and 1820s can be associated with an English tradition of colonnaded circular and octagonal tower stages dating from the London churches of Sir Christopher Wren: more specifically, the source for these towers seems to have been rooted in the scientific interest in archaeology of Wren and Nicholas Hawksmoor. Both these architects had turned to the Tower of the Winds for inspiration: Wren followed Cesariano's reconstruction of Vitruvius' description for St Mary Bride's, while Hawksmoor's design, a project for the main entrance of Worcester College, Oxford (possibly part of a scheme for a "Greek" Oxford), may have been known by Wyatt when he designed his tower for the same university some fifty years later.[15] As a scientist and member of the Royal Society, Wren is a probable connecting link between this institution, with its interest in archaeological expeditions, and in the designing of contemporary archi-tecture after archaeological reconstructions. There seems to have been a revival of interest in Wren contemporaneous with the early nineteenth-century archaeologically-inspired church towers. James Elmes, the archi-tect of the first tower of this group, began writing his *Memoires on the Life*

14. Examples are: Francis Bedford, St Luke's, West Norwood, Lambeth, 1822; H. E. Good-ridge, Tower for William Bedford, Lansdowne, Bath, 1825–1826; H. W. Reveley, St George's Cathedral, Cape Town, South Africa, 1830.

15. For St Mary Bride's tower, see Eduard F. Sekler, *Wren and His Place in European Architecture*, London, 1954, p. 105: for Oxford, see S. Lang, "Vanbrugh's Theory and Hawksmoor's Buildings", *JSAH*, XXIV, May 1965, p. 145: and for the Worcester College tower, see Kerry Downes, *Hawksmoor*, London, 1959, p. 397. The "Tower of Andromachus" (Tower of the Winds) was acknowledged by Hawksmoor to be the source for an early design for St Anne, Limehouse (Downes, ibid.).

F

and Works of Sir Christopher Wren in 1809,[16] and C. R. Cockerell, one of the joint authors of the supplementary fifth volume of the *Antiquities*, was interested in Wren's architecture, and published a pictorial selection of Wren's work as a *Tribute to the Memory of Sir Christopher Wren* in 1838.[17]

Stuart, curiously, was opposed to the imitation of archaeological discoveries. Joseph Papworth quoted him as replying to Sir Joshua Reynolds' compliment on the publication of the first volume of the *Antiquities*:

> Sir, . . . I undertook the labour in the hope to discover the *principles* on which the ancients proceeded, and I have drawn my own conclusions of them; but I fear, Sir Joshua, that many will be content to *copy* what they find detailed in this book, without regard to the *why* and *wherefore* that governed either the ancients or myself.

Papworth then noted: "The apprehension is verified by the practice of the day".[18]

Ornamental details from the archaeological publications also were adapted to contemporary architectural vocabulary. The *Palmyra* and *Balbec* Orders (Pl. 27) were already a part of standard French vocabulary developed from Perrault's Louvre façade, where the Balbec Order first may have been introduced.[19] But the sunflower motif from a ceiling published in *Palmyra* was used by Robert Adam at Osterley Park (Pls. 3, 4), and became a standard part of Neo-classical repertory.[20] In France, Jacques Germain Soufflot was influenced by the style of decorative material from *Palmyra* and *Balbec* in designing the Panthéon.[21] The standard Greek Ionic Order, first published in volume one of the *Antiquities of Athens* as the Order of the Temple of Ilissus (Pl. 28), and later repeated in the *Antiquities of Ionia*, became the Ionic norm of the Greek Revival, The severe semi-Corinthian Order of the Tower of the Winds, published in the first

16. Published in London, 1823.
17. See E. M. Dodd, "Charles Robert Cockerell", *Victorian Architecture*, ed. Farriday, London, 1963, pp. 111–112.
18. *Repository of Arts* . . . , ed. R. Ackermann, XIV, 2nd ser., 1 December 1822, p. 314.
19. See Chapter III, note 8.
20. This plate, from Wood's *Palmyra*, was one of those recommended by a French reviewer as unsuitable for use as a model (see Appendix II, entry 45).   21. See Appendix II, entry 56.

volume of the *Antiquities* (Pl. 29), and the Erechtheion Ionic Order, from the first edition of LeRoy s *Ruines* (Pl. 31), were adopted with modification by, for instance, Robert Adam at the Royal Society of Arts portico (Pl. 30), and in the Great Hall at Syon (Pl. 32). The similarity of the Tower of the Winds Order to Egyptian capitals, the ornamentation of the decorative band of the Erechtheion Order, and the possibilities for modification of both these Orders, caused them to merge into the ornamental vocabulary of the nineteenth century. And, finally, the ornamental and elegant Corinthian Order of the Monument of Lysicrates (Pl. 33) was used in formal interior spaces and on façades where special decorative emphasis was desired, such as Decimus Burton's Charing Cross Hospital (Pl. 34).[22]

In contrast to English absorption of material from the archaeological publications into traditional architectural currents, French use of archaeological material seems to have been without precedent and related to future developments. A contemporary French critic claimed that the Doric Orders from the Paestum temples were often used in Paris by younger architects, because of their "masculine proportions", and their ease of execution, but that it was difficult to classify these adaptations among the imitations of the Greek Orders, since they were subject to extensive modification, especially by Claude-Nicholas Ledoux. The critic further noted that, although the ancient examples were fluted in a particular manner, fluting was omitted by modern architects, probably for economical reasons.[23] Another explanation of the plain shafts was made

22. Examples of interiors are: William Brooks, School of Oriental Studies, London Institute, Finsbury Circus, London, 1815–1816; Henry Roberts, Fishmongers' Hall, London, 1831–1833. A version of this Order was used by Thomas and Lewis Cubitt at Eaton Square, London, 1827.

23. C. P. Landon, *Annales du Musée*, Paris, IX (1805), pp. 93–94: "Ce sont ces derniers [exemples de l'ordre Dorique dans les temples de Posidonie ou de Pestum] qui ont été vus et mesurés par la plupart des jeunes architectes, dans leur voyage d'Italie, qui ont mis cet ordre fort en usage à Paris depuis quelques années; ses proportions mâles, et la facilité que l'on a de l'exécuter sans le secours d'ornemens dispendieux, l'ont fait employer fréquemment; mais il ne l'avait encore été sur un aussi grand diamètre, car ceux qu'on voit aux pavillons des barrières, exécutés par M. Le Doux, ont reçu de cet architecte différents modifications, soit dans les profils, soit dans les proportions générales, qui empêchent de les classer parmi les imitations de l'Ordre des Grecs.

"On peut encore observer que dans les monumens antiques cet ordre est presque toujours cannelé d'une manière qui lui est particulière, et que l'économie sans doute a fait supprimer ses cannelures à la plupart de nos architectes modernes."

by LeRoy in a comparison of archaic Doric with Tuscan columns. LeRoy concluded that not only were the two Orders similar but that they must spring from the same origin.[24] LeRoy thus may have been the authority for the use of the baseless, unfluted columns which made a large contribution to Parisian architectural vocabulary during the last quarter of the eighteenth century.

The imaginative and varied examples of the baseless Doric Order often seen in French architecture after 1775, appeared first when Ledoux introduced baseless, bulging and unfluted columns on the entrance porch of his Salines at Arc-et-Senans (Pl. 35).[25] In the same year LeCamus de Mezières used a similar but slenderer version of this baseless unfluted Order on his Pagoda at Chanteloup (Pl. 36). LeCamus' version may have been related to LeRoy's plate of a slender, baseless Tuscan column from the Theatre of Marcellus in Rome, compared in the *Ruines* with a slender, fluted Greek Doric column (Pl. 40).

According to contemporary sources the most influential early Greek Doric structure in France was Joseph Antoine's porch for the Hôpital de la Charité (Pl. 38). Antoine's porch was credited with beginning the short-lived but widespread popularity in France of the Greek Doric Order,[26] a popularity which lasted for about twenty years. A critic noted the fact that Antoine's Order was not the correct Athenian Doric of Stuart

24. *Ruines*, 1758, Part 2, p. 3: "Ce parallele de l'Ordre Dorique . . . d'Athenes, & de l'Ordre Toscan . . . fait appercevoir tant de conformités entre ces deux Ordres, que nous ne doutons pas qu'ils n'ayent la même origine." LeRoy further developed this thesis in *Ruines*, 1770, p. 37. Piranesi reflected prevailing attitudes in his *Diverse maniere d'adornare i cammini . . .*, Rome, 1769, where he explained in "An Apologetical Essay in Defence of the Egyptian and Tuscan Architecture", that the two Orders, though developed separately, were "mixed together" by the Romans (p. 15), and further on classified the Tuscan and Doric capitals as identical (p. 23). See also note 31 below.

25. See Johannes Langner, "Ledoux und die 'Fabriques' ", *Zeitschrift für Kunstgeschichte*, XXVI, 1963, pp. 1–36. Langner further notes (p. 14) an earlier project by Soufflot for a Nymphaeum at Menars as having smooth-shafted baseless columns.

26. Quatremère de Quincy, *Vie des architectes*, Paris, 1830, II, pp. 324–325; "Ce petit monument, le premier du style dorique grec exécuté à Paris, est un des ouvrages qui firent le plus remarquer alors le talent d'Antoine, par les artistes et les gens de goût. Sans doute cet essai eût continué d'attirer l'attention si, au lieu d'une heureuse émulation entre les architectes et d'une application judicieuse aux monumens auxquels convient le caractère de cet ordre, une sorte de courant de mode n'en eût fait un emploi banal, sans mesure, sans discernement aucun, aux édifices les plus vulgaires, et jusqu'à en rendre l'aspect insignifiant et même fastidieux."

(doubtless referring to the Parthenon and Hephaesteion published in the second and third volumes of the *Antiquities*): the columns were truncated and the capitals overpowering.[27] Antoine's Order seems to be similar to the archaic Orders of Paestum, but LeRoy was cited as the source:[28] and, to be sure, the relatively high pediment of the portico is related to that of the so-called "Temple of Augustus", or main portico of the Roman forum in Athens (Pl. 37), published in LeRoy's *Ruines*. The unclassical proportions of the Order may be due to the fact that LeRoy did include examples of the archaic Orders in his *Ruines*; he had intended to publish material from Paestum in this book.[29] Another deviation from the "correct" Greek Doric Order in Antoine's portico was not mentioned by any critic: the corner triglyph was placed directly over the corner column, and not at the end of the frieze, a traditional solution which would be standard for the remainder of the eighteenth century.

During the 1780s and 1790s variations of this baseless Order were used extensively in French architecture, generally without fluting. They appeared where, for aesthetic, financial, or utilitarian reasons, a strong, simple statement was needed, such as in the courtyard of a Parisian house (Pl. 41), the cloister of a convent (where the court was compared to the monuments of Paestum while the Order was considered Tuscan) (Pl. 42),[30] the dance hall of a working-class pleasure garden (Pl. 43), and a late

27. Comte de Saint-Victor, *Tableau historique et pittoresque de Paris* . . ., Paris, 1811, III, p. 774, note 1: "Cette représentation des propylées parut assez fidèle à ceux qui ne les connoissoient que superficelliement, et par les dessins qui en furent donnés dans le temps; mais ceux qui avoient étudié l'ouvrage alors très peu connu de Stuart, regrettèrent qu'on eut ainsi tronqué les proportions de l'original, en élevant le fronton, en retranchant sur l'architrave, en négligeant plusiers détails dans les profils: les chapiteaux, trop saillants, n'ont point le caractère de l'antique; les triglyphes sont trop longs; en un mot, ce seroit prendre une très fausse idée de la sévérité, de la grace et de l'harmonie de l'ordre des propylées que de le juger sur ce petit monument."

28. Quatremère de Quincy, work cited in note 26 above, p. 324: "Les esquisses que David le Roi venait aussi de communiquer aux artistes, sur les monumens d'Athènes, enhardirent notre architecte [Antoine], et bientôt on vit un portique de quatre colonnes sans bases, avec les principaux caractères de l'ordre antique, dans ses détails, dans ses cannelures, dans sa frise et dans son fronton." See also J. G. Legrand, *Description de Paris* . . ., Paris, 1806, I, p. 135. Quatremère de Quincy (ibid., II, p. 323) also commented on the orientation of this Order to Paestum, mentioning prior knowledge of the work of Gazola in Paris.   29. See Appendix I, entry K.

30. Now Lycée Condorcet, 8 rue de Havre. For the association with Paestum, see Luc Vincent Thiery, *Guide des amateurs* . . . *à Paris*, Paris, 1787, II, p. 139; and Saint-Victor, work cited in note 27 above, II, p. 138.

fluted example in a projected Bourse (Pl. 44). One interesting variant of this Order was that of the Temple of Apollo at Delos in which fluting was indicated at the top and base of what was otherwise a Tuscan shaft. It was published in LeRoy's *Ruines* (Pl. 39) and was known also by Revett. LeRoy considered that this Order further supported his contention that the Paestum and Tuscan Orders had a similar origin.[31] It appeared in examples between *c.* 1776, when Revett incorporated the Order in the East portico of Trafalgar House, Wilts. (Pl. 45), and 1819, when C. R. Cockerell adapted it to the garden façade at Oakley Park, Salop. A possibly unique example in France of this unusual Order occurred on the garden facade of J. N. Durand's one building, the Maison de la Thuille, in Paris (Pl. 46).

The baseless Greek Doric Order, with and without fluting, was introduced in English architecture soon after its appearance in France. Sir John Soane (who had visited Paestum in 1779[32]) began designing variations on this Order almost from the moment the variants on the Order were introduced in France. The columns of his first essay in this Order, a project for a Triumphal Bridge, designed in 1776,[33] are slender (possibly influenced by material from LeRoy); those of his 1778 Residence for a Canine Family (Pl. 48) are squat and heavy, and seem to be closest to the archaic Order of one of the Temples at Paestum, published by Major (Pl. 47). The baseless Doric Order was used mainly by Soane[34] in England prior to the nineteenth century. However, the Order was found occasionally in the work of other English architects, and its first appearance in England may have been with the unfluted, engaged columns of

31. *Ruines*, 1758, Part 2, p. 5: "Cette ressemblance . . . entre l'Ordre Toscan & les Ordres Doriques de Grece de la première antiquité . . . est encore confirmé par les profils des colonnes du célèbre Temple d'Apollon . . ."

32. A sketchbook containing notes Soane made on his journey to Paestum is on deposit at the Soane Museum.

33. See Dorothy Stroud, "Soane's Designs for a Triumphal Bridge", *AR*, CXXI, April 1957, pp. 261–262.

34. Examples of baseless columns by Soane can be found at, for instance, Sydney Lodge, Moggerhanger, Tyringham, and Bentley Priory. For illustrations, see Dorothy Stroud, *The Architecture of Sir John Soane*, London, 1961.

Thomas Johnson's Warwick Gaol, 1779–1783 (Pl. 49).[35] The columns of Soane's Barn à la Paestum at Solihull (Pl. 50),[36] are similarly unfluted, as was one of the final versions of this Order, George Dance's Stratton Park portico, of 1803 (Pl. 51).

The widespread popularity of this Order and its variations can be estimated from the extent of Chambers' reaction to it in 1791 in his *Treatise on Civil Architecture*. Here he repeated his earlier statement against the "deformities" of "Grecian buildings" and deplored the recent introduction of the "Gusto Greco" into English architecture.[37] In 1794 Willey Reveley noted that Chambers could only be referring to the architecture of Paestum,[38] and, indeed, by the 1790s many of the variations on the baseless Doric Order were related closely to the Paestum monuments. An Order from Major's *Paestum* (Pl. 52) occurs in a rare instance on the garden façade of Benjamin Latrobe's Hammerwood House (Pl. 53): only the lack of fluting on the shaft differs from the original model.[39] In Joseph Bonomi's church at Great Packington (Pl. 55), the columns seem to follow Chambers' exaggerated description of the "gouty" columns of Paestum, and are close to an Order illustrated in Major's *Paestum* (Pl. 54). The fluted shafts and flattened capitals of Soane's romantic 1790 project for a sepulchral chapel at Tyringham (Pl. 56) and his 1807 project for a tomb for Francis Bourgeois (Pl. 57) also are close to the Paestum Orders.

The unfluted archaic Greek Doric Order of the eighteenth century was composed of material assimilated from many sources, and subjected to unorthodox solutions. In spite of the fact that accurately measured illustrations of classical Athenian monuments were available during this period, there was no reference to them. Instead, the concept of a baseless

35. Information on the Gaol is in Arthur Oswald, "Georgian Warwick—II", *Country Life*, CX, 26 October 1951, pp. 1378–1379. According to Oswald, the columns originally were intended to be fluted.

36. See Dorothy Stroud, "Soane Barn", *AR*, CXIX, June 1956, pp. 336–337.

37. W. Chambers, *Treatise* . . . , London, 1791 (3rd ed.), pp. 23–24, 26.

38. *AA*, III (1794), p. xiii, note b.

39. C. D. Lewis, *The Influence of Archaeological Publications in the Emergence of a Greek Revival Style: 1759–1809*, unpublished B. A. thesis, School of Architecture, Cambridge, 1962, has previously commented on the similarity of the Hammerwood Order to that of Paestum.

Doric Order was in character with the spirit of permissive licence of the first volume of the *Antiquities*. Indeed, it may be that the first French edition of the *Antiquities*, published in London in 1793, repeating the entire format and plates of the original first volume, was brought out to capitalize on this trend in taste in France.

The sudden imitation and adaptation of unorthodox antique models may have been related to mid-eighteenth century emphasis on a return to the "sources" of architecture by, for instance, the Abbé Laugier. Desire to restrict architecture to the essential components of the post and lintel system and the rustic hut may have stimulated interest in preclassical models such as those of Paestum. However, it should not be forgotten that French architectural reform was begun before the publication of the archaeological studies of the Levant and Paestum, and that the French concept of "Greek", whatever immediate form it took, was part of a continuous tradition.[40] French architectural theory did not deviate from its tradition even when closely connected with the English archaeological movement. LeRoy said that his work was intended to bring to light the first principles of architecture, and not to be a source for specific details or accurate measurements. Soufflot, in spite of his association with Paestum, was interested in the application of the principles associated with Greek architecture and not in the archaeologically correct forms.[41]

Against this background the pamphlet by Thomas Hope, recommending the classical Greek Doric Order for the new Downing College, Cambridge, was published in 1804.[42] Hope was influenced by eighteenth-century French developments; he wished to rival recent French architecture,[43] and, like Laugier, he specifically endorsed the wooden hut and banned pilasters.[44] Moreover, Hope recognized that the Greek Doric Order still was considered abnormal, for he permitted bases for the

40. W. Herrmann, *Laugier . . .* , London, 1962, esp. pp. 35–52.
41. Jean Monval, *Soufflot, sa vie—Son oeuvre—Son esthétique (1713–1780)*, Paris, 1918, pp.491–505, esp. Soufflot's *Mémoire* delivered at the Academy of Lyon, 9 September 1744.
42. Thomas Hope, *Observations on the Plans and Elevations Designed by James Wyatt, Architect, for Downing College, Cambridge . . .* , London, 1804.
43. Ibid., p. 35.
44. Ibid., p. 20, for the wooden hut; p. 28, for banning pilasters.

columns.[45] However, he endorsed the Athenian models of the Parthenon and the Hephaesteion; models which had been ignored previously, but which would become the Doric norm for nineteenth-century Greek Revival architecture.[46]

In 1809, five years after the publication of Hope's pamphlet, the "correct" baseless Greek Doric, illustrated in the second and third volumes of the *Antiquities of Athens*, appeared on one of the most extreme statements of the Greek Revival—the subordination of a country house to a Greek temple front designed by William Wilkins at Grange Park, Alresford, Hampshire. The façade was closely modelled after the Hephaesteion at Athens (Pls. 58, 59), even to the correct relationship of the triglyph to the corner of the frieze, a relationship which now occurred on a permanent, monumental, European structure, possibly for the first time.[47] From now on, through the first quarter of the nineteenth century, and lingering into the second quarter, the "correct" classical Greek Doric Order would become accepted as an architectural norm.

The concept of the single norm of the classical Greek temple, applied to as many building types as possible, became the most criticized element of the Greek Revival when this norm could no longer fulfil the more complex architectural needs of the later nineteenth century. Although the variety and licence of the first volume of the *Antiquities* predicted trends in nineteenth-century architecture, as a publication it was classified with the later volumes and rejected when the Greek Revival waned. As early as 1822 Joseph Papworth spoke out strongly against the publications of the *Antiquities*, saying:

. . . originality is wholly disregarded. The Parthenon and temple of Minerva Polias, the Choragic monuments, the tower of Andronicus; in fact, the contents of Stuart's and Revett's *Antiquities of Athens* are over

45. Thomas Hope, *Observations on the Plans and Elevations Designed by James Wyatt, Architect*, p. 22.
46. Ibid., pp. 17, 21.
47. Corner triglyphs were correctly located on earlier garden structures: examples are, Stuart's Temples at Hagley Park and Shugborough and Soane's project for a Chapel at Tyringham.

and over again copied for any and every purpose, and with these the public are satisfied; and so long as the error endures, any man by that work may set up for an architect, fearless of public condemnation.[48]

But during the reaction against the strict limitation of the Greek Revival, admiration for classical Greece remained; now critics turned from advocating specific imitation to emulation of the spirit of Greek architecture. In 1847 James Elmes, in a short history of architecture, maintained that the beauty of Greek architecture, which Stuart and Revett first captured for the European world, lay in the free-hand drawing of the Greek architects which, contrasted to "clumsy", "mechanical" Roman detailing, was intuitive, artistic, and therefore more beautiful.[49] And, as if in tribute to the continuing vitality of this extraordinary publication, an edition of the *Antiquities* appeared in 1881.[50] It was published in French, in a series of line drawings, reduced in size, with no text, but with a list of corrections included in the table of contents. Its editor was J. J. Hittdorff, whose namesake, by his archaeological researches, had noted earlier the use of colour in ancient temples, and thus established a precedent for the painted exteriors of contemporary structures in the same manner that Stuart's first volume became the archaeological excuse for the creative liberties of his own generation.

48. *Repository of Arts . . .*, ed. R. Ackermann, XIV, 2nd ser., 1 December 1822, pp. 313–314.

49. James Elmes, "History of Architecture in Great Britain", *Civil Engineer and Architect's Journal*, X, 1847, p. 339.

50. There is a later publication of the *Antiquities* material: *Griechische Baukunst nach J. Stuart u. N. Revett*, Berlin, 1922, with an introduction by Cornelius Gurlitt, containing reduced plates of outstanding monuments from the first three volumes.

APPENDIX I

PROPOSALS, ETC., FOR THE ARCHAEOLOGICAL PUBLICATIONS

Contents

I. Proposals for the Antiquities of Athens

I. Proposals for the Antiquities of Athens

ROME PROPOSALS

A. 1748 PROPOSAL (mentioned, *AA*, I, p.v.)

B. 1749 (6 January) PROPOSAL (summarized from a lost letter from Revett to his father, *AA*, IV, pp. xxix–xxx: probably the same as the lost proposal drafted by Revett with corrections by Stuart mentioned in BM, MS Add. 22.152, p. 6, entry L):

The first mention of visiting and drawing the antiquities of Athens, occurs in a letter to his [Revett's] father, dated January 6 1749. The scheme originated with Mr. Revett and Mr. Gavin Hamilton; and their knowledge of the temper, talents, acquirements, and reputation of Stuart, induced them to persuade him to join them in an undertaking from which, in the enthusiasm of youthful hope, they promised themselves pleasure, honour, and great emoluments.

The work was to consist of three volumes; the first to contain fifty-three views of the country and its edifices; the second, plans, elevations and architectural details, occupying seventy-one plates; the third was expected to contain sixty-seven plates of sculpture. The whole was to be completed in four years, the Artists engraving most of the subjects themselves after their return to England, which they imagined would be in about one year from leaving Rome; and the neat profit at the end of the four years to the three Artists was, at the most *moderate compensation*, and after paying every expense while thus employed, to amount to ten thousand pounds; and they thought it probable that it would ultimately produce three times that sum, though they were aware that the latter portions would come in slowly.

VENICE PROPOSALS

C. 1751 PROPOSAL (BM, MS 6210 fol. 96: printed in *Original Letters of Eminent Literary Men*, ed. Henry Ellis, London, 1843, pp. 379–389), Thomas Hollis to John Ward, 26 February 1751:

(a) *Explanatory Letter*

According to the promise which I made when in England, of acquainting you with any thing that fell in my way abroad that I should think worthy of your notice, I take the liberty of sending you the present Letter, with the enclosed Proposals, and account of a Scheme for taking and publishing the Antiquities existing at Athens and its neighbourhood, &c. &c. by Mr. Stuart and Mr. Rivet, Englishmen, and painters and architects. Mr. Stuart and Mr. Rivet are both of them young men of about thirty years of age, who have been, as I am informed, in Italy, and chiefly at Rome, upwards of ten years, where they applied themselves closely to their studies, and where Mr. Stuart in particular distinguished himself in divers respects, among others by a Treatise which he wrote upon Obelisques, (dedicated to the now Marquis of Rockingham, his great patron,) which was thought a very ingenious performance. Near a year since they came to Venice, intending to have gone from thence at that time into Greece, but could not meet with a firm opportunity till about a month ago, when (together with an under-assistant) they embarqued aboard an English vessel for Zant, in the way to Athens. When they went away, they imagined it would take them up to about eight months to execute what is to be done in Attica: but as they are men of the greatest accuracy and exactness, and that they may find out more matter than as yet they can be informed of, it is probable it will take up a longer time. If they can enjoy their healths there, and they execute this first scheme without interruption from the Turks (of which there is some danger, not withstanding that they have recommendatory Letters to all the principal persons of the places where they are to go to, and that they are furnished with the Grand Signor's firman, which Mr. Porter our ambassador obtained for them), it is not impossible that they may be tempted afterwards to take Plans of some other considerable Antiquities that are in other parts of Greece. It is very desirable that Mr. Stuart and Mr. Rivet should go through with their Design in its most extensive manner, because they are believed in all respects equal to the work, especially since what they have done in Pola, and because however beautiful and considerable these Antiquities are, yet the Designs that have been taken of them hitherto, have been rather Sketches, they say, than accurate and exact Plans such as theirs will be. Here at Venice they were much taken notice of, and encouraged in their undertaking by the Resident Sir James Gray, and the Consul, Mr. Smith, who are both of them ingenious and learned Gentlemen, and by the English gentlemen in general that passed this way, who have given their names to the Work; and they have likewise had promises of subscriptions, when they take them in in form, from several people of the first distinction in Italy. As it is possible you may not yet have heard of this undertaking even generally, and as it is probable that you have not seen the particulars of it, I could not forbear writing to you concerning it, and desiring for you, of Mr. Stuart, the inclosed scheme of it, imagining it would not be unacceptable to you, and I am certain if, upon knowing of it, you should be willing to enter into a correspondence with Mr. Stuart in respect to it, he would think it an honor, and much to his advantage. In case that will be agreeable to you, you will please to direct to him at Joseph Smith, Esq., His Brittanic Majesty's Consul at Venice, who will forward the Letter, there being continually Vessels going from thence into Greece. . . .

(b) *The Proposal*
Proposals for publishing a new and accurate Description of the Antiquities, &c. in the Province of Attica by James Stuart and Nicholas Revett.

There is perhaps no part of Europe more deservedly excites the Curiosity and Attention of the lovers of Polite Literature than the Province of Attica, and in particular Athens its capital City; whether we reflect on the figure it makes in History, on account of the excellent Men it has produced, or whether we consider the number of Antiquities still remaining there, monuments of the good sense and elevated genius of the Athenians, and the most perfect Models of what is excellent in Sculpture and Architecture.

Many Authors have mentioned these remains of Antiquity, as Works of great magnificence, and most exquisite taste; but their Descriptions are so confused, and their Measures so inaccurate, that the most expert Architect could not from these Books form an idea distinct enough to make exact Drawings of any one building they describe. Their works seem rather calculated to raise our admiration than to satisfy our curiosity, or improve our taste.

Rome, who borrowed her Arts and frequently her Artificers from Greece, has by means of Serlio, Palladio, Santo Bartoli, and other ingenious men, preserved the memory of the most excellent Sculptures, and magnificent Edifices which once adorned her; and though some of the originals are since destroyed, yet the memory, the exact form of these things, nay the Arts themselves seem secured from perishing, since the industry of these men have dispersed examples of them through all the Polite Nations of Europe.

But Athens, the mother of Elegance and Politeness, whose magnificence scarce yielded to that of Rome, and who for the beauties of a correct style must be allowed to surpass her, as much as an original excels a copy, has been almost entirely neglected, and unless exact drawings from them be speedily made, all her beauteous Fabricks, her Temples, her Theatres, her Palaces will drop into oblivion, and Posterity will have to reproach us, that we have not left them a tolerable idea of what is so excellent, and so much deserves our attention. The reason indeed of this neglect is obvious.

Greece, since the Revival of the Arts, has been in the possession of Barbarians. And Artificers capable of such a Work have been able to gratify their passion for fame or profit, without risking themselves among such professed enemies to the Arts, as the Turks still are, and whose ignorance and jealousy make an Undertaking of this sort still somewhat dangerous.

While those Gentlemen who have travelled there, though some of them have been abundantly furnished with Literature, yet have not any of them been sufficiently conversant with Painting, Sculpture, and Architecture, to make their Books of such general use, or even entertainment to the Public, as a man more acquainted with those Arts might do; for the best verbal Descriptions cannot be supposed to convey so adequate an idea of the magnificence and elegance of Buildings, the fine form, expression or proportion of Sculptures, the beauty or variety of a country, or the exact scene of any celebrated Action, as may be formed from Drawings made on the spot, measured with the greatest accuracy, and delineated with the utmost attention.

We doubt not but a Work so much wanted will meet with the Approbation of all those Gentlemen who are lovers of Antiquity, or have a taste for what is excellent in these Arts, as we are assured that those Artists who aim at perfection must be infinitely more pleased, and better instructed, the nearer they can draw their examples from the fountain-head.

It is proposed to divide this book into three Volumes, the first of which will consist of Views of the principal Antiquities in their present state, and Prospects of those places mentioned by Poets and Historians, either on account of the beautiful situation, or as the Scenes of any celebrated Action, together with an exact Map of all the Provinces of Attica trigonometrically surveyed.

The second Volume will contain the Geometrical Plans and Elevations of the Temples, Theatres, &c. still remaining there, after the manner of Desgodetz, in which will be given, with the greatest accuracy, the measure and proportion of each particular member, as well as the general disposition and ordonance of the whole Building, restored to its original form, whenever materials can be found for such a restoration, for the justness and probability of which (it is to be observed) the first Volume will be a sufficient voucher. And to this Volume will be prefixed a Plan of Modern Athens, with so much of the adjacent Country as may be supposed to have been contained within the ancient Walls.

The third Volume will consist of Statues and Basso Relievos still remaining there, many of which are supposed to be the work of Phidias, Praxiteles, and other most excellent Sculptors; of all which the following Catalogue will give a more particular Idea.

	Tom. 1st. Views.	Tom. 2d. Archi:	Tom. 3d. Basso Relievos.
The Temple of Minerva Parthenion, Doric order enriched with Sculptures	2	8	20
Temple of Victory without Wings, Doric Order	1	2	6
Arsenal of Lycurgus, Ionic Order	1	3	
Temple of Erectheus, Ionic Order	1	3	
of Minerva and the Nymph Pandrosa with Caryatides	1	2	4
of Pan and Apollo, Corinthian Order	1	1	
Theatre of Bacchus, three Orders	2	8	
Portico of Eumenes	1	1	
Palace of Hadrian, Corinthian Order	5	6	
Acqueduct of Hadrian, Ionic Order	2	2	
Gate of Hadrian	2	3	
Temple of Diana Agrotera	1	2	
Stadium Panathenaicum	1	2	
Antique Bridge on Illisus	1	2	
Temple of Ceres	1	1	
Temple of the Muses Illisiades	1		
An Antique Temple, now a Church, called Hagia Maria	1	1	
The Museum	1	2	
Odeum	1	2	
The Fountain Henneacrene	1		
The Church of St. Dennis the Areopagite	1		
Temple of Theseus, Doric Order, enriched with Sculptures	1	6	20
Gymnasium of Ptolemy	2	1	
Temple of Castor and Pollux	1	2	
The Lyceum	1		
Temple of Augustus, Corinthian Order	1	3	
of Jupiter Olympus, Corinthian Order	2	5	
Tower of the Eight Winds, built by Andronicus Cyrrestes	1	1	8
Lanthorn of Demosthenes, Corinthian Order, Enriched with Sculptures	1	4	10
The Pyreum, or Ancient Port of Athens	1		
The Μακρα Τειχη	1		
Temple of Diana Munychia	1	2	
of Jupiter at Salamis	1	3	

	Tom. 1st. *Views.*	*Tom.* 2^d. *Archi:*	*Tom.* 3^d. *Basso Relievos.*
of Venus at Egina	I	2	
of Ceres at Eleusis	I	3	5
An ancient Temple at Eleusis, now the Church of Saint George	I	I	
An octagon Temple near Corinth, adorned with sculptures	I	2	8
Temple of Minerva at Sunium	I	2	
Rupes Scironides	I		
Views of Athens, Megara, Eleusis, Mt Cytheron, Helicon, Mt Parnassus, Mt Hymettus, Pentelicus, Leuctra, Marathon, Platea, and Salamis	12		
A Map of the Province of Attica	2		
A Plan of Athens		2	
	62	90	83

These are the Subjects which we propose to ourselves, after consulting the Writings of the most creditable Authors, and conversing with several Gentlemen who have visited this Country. It is possible nevertheless that, on our arrival there, we shall be obliged to omitt some, that by the injuries of Time will be entirely ruin'd, and we may add others of which we cannot yet be supposed to have any Notice. We shall likewise endeavour, though in the concisest manner possible, to illustrate each Print with such explanations and descriptions as will be necessary to make them useful, and intelligible, which will be chiefly done by pointing out the relation they may have to the Doctrine of Vitruvius, or the Description of Pausanias, Strabo, &c.

During the time we waited at Venice for an embarkation to Zant, least so much time should be unemployed, we resolved to make a little voyage to Pola in Istria; assuring ourselves, on the judgment of Palladio, that we should find in that place some Antiquities deserving our notice. 'At Pola (says he) in Istria, besides the Theatre and Ampihtheatre, and an Arch, which are the most beautiful Buildings, &c. there are on one side of the Piazza two Temples', &c. Pall. Archit. lib. 4. Nor were we deceived in our expectation; for, though the Theatre be entirely destroyed yet the Arch of the Sergii, the outward precinct of an Amphitheatre in excellent preservation, and a Temple built in the most exquisite taste of the Augustan Age, were sufficient materials to keep us continually employed three months, much to our advantage and instruction; for by discovering the mistakes which Serlio, Palladio, and Maffei have committed in what regards this place, we are convinced of the necessity of using all our diligence in measuring and designing whatever

Antiquities may fall under our notice, as it is doubtless owing to inaccuracy, and the too cursory view which these great men have bestowed on the Antiquities of Pola, that they have succeeded so ill in their representations of them. They seem neither to have dug, nor to have raised the necessary scaffolds.

It may not be amiss before we conclude, to observe that a greater number of Examples than those we already have, are necessary in order to form a true judgment of the ancient Architecture; for though many Treatises on this subject have been published, it cannot be truly said we have any Author except Desgodetz, on whose authenticity we can entirely depend; and although his Book contains many excellent Examples of the Corinthian Order, yet unless the Coliseo and the Theatre of Marcellus can be supposed Models fit for our imitation in Buildings of a less gigantic structure, he must be allowed to be very deficient in what regards the Doric and Ionic Orders, as he gives us no Temple of the first, and of the second only that dedicated to Manly Fortune.

Of the Antiquities of Pola we have made the following Designs:

Of the Amphitheatre

1. An External View ⎱ which shews exactly the present condition of
2. An Internal Ditto ⎰ this Building
3. A Plan.
4. A General Elevation of the Front, with a transverse Section.
5. An Elevation of one of the Abutments, called by Serlio contraforti.
6. An Elevation of a Flank of Ditto, with Profils of some cornices belonging to them, &c.
7. Sections, &c. of Ditto, shewing their Use.
8. A Plan and Elevation of two Piers of Basement.
9. Zoccolo, Cornice, &c. of Ditto.
10. A Plan, Elevation of Arch of the first Order.
11. Capital, Entablature and Impost of Ditto.
12. A Plan and Elevation of an Arch of the Second Order.
13. Capital, Entablature and Impost of Ditto.
14. A Plan and Elevation of Part of the Upper Order, shewing one Window, the Channels and Zoccolos, in which the poles were planted, that the Vail was fastened to.
15. A Section of the Upper Cornice, and of the Architrave and Cornice of the Windows, &c.

Of the Arch

16. A View shewing the situation and condition it is now in.
17. A Plan.
18. An Elevation of the Front.
19. Ditto of the Flank.
20. A Section.

G

21. Basement and Base of the Columns.
22. Capital and Entablature, with a profil of the Capital.
23. Angular View and Plan of Capital.
24. The Attick Story, Impost of the Arch, and a Basso Relievo representing an Eagle, with the wings extended, grasping a Serpent, in the suffit of the Arch.

Of the Temple
26. A view of the Front, shewing the condition it is now in.
27. Ditto of the Back Front, with another consimilar Temple.
28. A Plan.
29. An Elevation of the Front.
30. Ditto of the Flank.
31. Basement and Base of the Columns, with Foliages that adorn the Frieze.
32. Capital and Entablature, with a Profil of the Capital.
33. An angular View and Plan of ditto.
34. Capital of the Pilasters. Its Profil and Plan. Soffit of the Architrave, and Base of the Pilasters.

D. 1751 PROPOSAL (text printed in full in *AA*, I, pp. v–vi, note a: issued by Colonel George Gray, London). The Proposal repeats Proposal C with slight editorial changes (see Appendix II, entry 4). However, the Catalogue is considerably altered from Proposal C, and may reflect changes occurring after Proposal C was originally issued (see also Proposals E, F, and especially G):

Catalogue of 1751 proposal:

First Volume	*Views*	*Architecture*	*Sculpture*
A large View of the Acropolis	1		
A general Plan of the antiquities included in this Volume		1	
The Propylaea, Temple of Victory, &c. Doric and Ionic	1	10	
The Doric Temple of Minerva Parthenion, enriched with Sculpture	2	9	50
The Ionic Temples of Minerva Polias, and Erechtheus and that of Pandrosus, adorned with Caryatides	2	20	4
The Theatre of Bacchus	1	4	
The Church of the Panagia Spiliotissa	1	4	4
	8	48	58

	Views	Architecture	Sculpture
Second Volume			
A large View of the City of Athens	I		
A Plan of the remains of the ancient City		I	
A Chart of the three Ports of Athens		I	
The Temple of Jupiter Olympus, Corinthian Order	I	10	
The Temple of Augustus, Doric Order	I	5	
The Temple of Theseus, Doric Order enriched with Sculpture	I	8	12
The Temple of Ceres, Ionic Order	I	7	
The Odeum of Herodes Atticus, or of Regilla		I	
The Monument of Philopappus, Corinthian Order	I	7	3
The Tower of the Winds enriched with Sculptures	I	6	8
The Lanthorn of Demosthenes, enriched with Sculptures	I	7	14
The Arch of Hadrian, Corinthian Order	I	9	
The Columns of Hadrian, Corinthian Order	I	4	
The Antique Bridge on the Ilissus	I		
The Acqueduct of Adrian, Ionic Order	I	4	
	12	70	37

Third Volume

The antiquities of Eleusis, Megara, Sunium, etc.

ATHENS PROPOSALS

E. 1752 PROPOSAL (mentioned in *AA*, I, p. v: issued by Samuel Ball, London). According to Appendix II, entry 4, the 1752 Proposal was "effectively the same as . . . [Proposal C], though somewhat more methodized".

F. n.d. (mentioned in *AA*, I, p. v: repetition of Proposal D with the deletion of one paragraph; issued by Wood and Dawkins).

G. 1752 (30 September) PROPOSAL (translation and abstraction in *JB*, X, January–February 1753, pp. 165–172):
Mémoire sur une nouvelle description des Antiquités qui se trouvent à Athènes & dans les environs.

On se flatte que l'Auteur de ce Journal ne refusera point une place à l'Ecrit qu'on lui envoye. Ceux, de qui il vient, méritent à tous égards, qu'on s'intéresse à eux & à leur Ouvrage. Leurs talens sont connus, & c'est le desir de se rendre utiles qui leur a fait entre-prendre cette tache pénible. Ils luttent depuis deux ans contre la jalousie, l'ignorance, & l'avarice des habitans de la ville autrefois la plus polie. C'est par un bonheur singulier qu'ils ont jusqu'ici soutenu les difficultés & les dangers de leur entreprise; & l'entière exécution dépend & de la continuation de ce bonheur, & des encouragemens du Public. On leur a déja procuré ici trois cent souscriptions, & l'on se flatte d'en recevoir de tous les lieux, où le gout des arts, de l'élégance, & des lettres n'est pas tout-à-fait étient.

D'Athènes le 30 de Septembre 1752.

La description nouvelle & exacte de toutes les antiquités, qui se trouvent à Athènes & dans la Province de l'Attique, commencée par nous Jaques Stuart & Nicolas Revett en 1751, étant actuellement considérablement avancée, nous nous voyons en état de donner une idée complette de tout l'Ouvrage.

Il consistera en vues, qui représenteront fidèlement l'état présent du pais, & de ses Antiquités, avec des Plans géometriques & des profils de ces Antiquités suivant la methode de Des Godetz. On y marquera avec la plus grande exactitude la mesure & les proportions de chaque membre particulier, la disposition & l'ordonnance générale des édifices entiers, & celles des statues & des bas-reliefs. Il en reste un grand nombre de très curieux tant pour le sujet que pour l'exécution. Nouse donnerons aussi des Cartes & des Plans pour marquer la situation générale & la liaison de tout l'ouvrage. Tout ceci sera compris en trois volumes *in folio* dont voici la disposition.

Le premier volume contiendra les Antiquités de l'Acropolis, le second celles de la ville, & le troisième sera pour les morceaux dispersés en divers endroits du territoire d'Athènes. Le catalogue que nous joignons à ce mémoire donnera une idée distincte du tout. Nous nous efforcerons d'éclaircir chaque planche par une explication concise propre à les rendre intelligibles & utiles. C'est ce que nous ferons principalement en marquant le rapport qui s'y trouve avec la doctrine de Vitruve ou avec les descriptions de Pausanias, de Strabon, &c.

Nous avons actuellement fini plus de la moitié de l'ouvrage, & nous acheverons avec toute la diligence possible le reste de notre laborieuse tâche. Il est impossible de fixer dès à-présent le prix de la souscription. Le grand nombre de planches, à l'exécution desquelles les meilleurs graveurs seront employés, nous engageront à de très grands frais. La souscription ne pourra par conséquent être que haute, & le moindre prix de chaque exemplaire sera de 10 ou 12£ st. Chaque planche ne reviendra pas à 9 sols à nos souscripteurs, quoique la beauté & la grandeur de plusieurs d'entr'elles égalent celles des planches qu'on vend cinq ou six shelings.

Remarquez que dans le Catalogue suivant la première colonne des chifres marque le nombre des vues, la seconde celui des planches d'architecture, & la troisième le nombre des statues & des bas reliefs que l'édifice qui les contient fournira.

[The first two volumes of the Catalogue are similar to Proposal D except for some minor changes in format: Propylaea, 4 bas-reliefs omitted; Lantern of Demosthenes, 2 bas-reliefs added; Fountain of Callirhoe, 1 view added; Bridge over Ilissus, architectural details omitted.]

Troisieme Volume

Les Antiquités d'Eleusis, de Mégare, de Sunium &c. avec des plans particuliers de Marathon, de Panorme &c. On y ajoutera un plan mesuré de toute la province de l'Attique, quelques antiquités qui se trouvent en différentes parties de la grece, & si nos souscripteurs ne s'y opposent point, trente quatre planches des Antiquités de Pole en Istrie.

G1. n.d. (*AA*, IV, Preface, p. i: ". . . in some of the early printed proposals the Antiquities of Pola are mentioned as the subject of the second volume".)

H. 1753 PROPOSAL (mentioned in *AA*, I, p. v: issued by Joseph Smith, Venice. Dispersed in various parts of Europe.)

LATER PROPOSALS

I. May 1754 letter (now lost), Stuart and Revett probably to Sir James Porter (mentioned in *AA*, IV, p. xvii) noting their intention to publish only the Monument to Lysicrates and the Tower of the Winds in a first volume.

J. 1755 PROPOSAL (mentioned in *AA*, I, p. v, note a): "Since our return to England we have found it convenient, to make some change in the disposition, which we had originally intended to give this Work. This change was specified in the Proposals published by us at London, January 1755."

II. Proposal for Ruines . . . de la Grèce

K. 1756 PROPOSAL text printed, probably in full, with commentary, in *AL*, 20 March 1756, II, pp. 22–31):

Les Ruines des plus beaux Monumens de la Grèce ou Recueil de dessins & de vûes de ces Monumens, avec leur histoire, & des réfléxions sur les progrès de l'Architecture.

Ce grand ouvrage sera divisé en deux Parties. Dans la première, on envisagera les Monumens du côté historique; dans la seconde, on les considérera du côté de l'Architecture, c'est-à-dire, par rapport à leurs proportions, à leurs mesures, &c. La première partie contiendra trois plans généraux de *Sparte*, d'*Athènes* & de la citadelle d'*Athènes*. Le plan de *Sparte* & de la plaine qui l'environne comprendra la nouvelle ville de *Mistra*, une partie du fleuve *Eurotas*, les ruisseaux de *Gnacion* & de *Babyca*. Les positions des anciennes villes d'*Amyclée* & de *Thérapnée* y seront aussi marquées. Au plan de la citadelle d'Athènes & à celui d'Athènes même & de toute la plaine qui s'étend depuis les montagnes de *Corydalies* & de *Pentilicus* jusqu'à la mer, on ajoûtera une Carte des ports de Pirée, de *Phalère*, de *Munychie*, & du fameux détroit de *Salamines*. Il y aura de plus dans cette première partie 25 vûes de Monumens particuliers; scavoir, pour *Athènes*, ceux du Temple de *Jupiter Olympien*, de la *Tour des Vents*, de la *Lanterne de Démosthène*, de l'*Arc de Philopappus*, du *Portique de*

Thésée, du *Panthéon d'Adrien*, du *Temple d'Auguste*, du *Stade*, de l'*Aréopage* & de l'*Odéon*, du *Temple de Minerve Suniade*, du *Temple de Thésée*, d'un *Temple de la Bourgade de Zoter*, pour la citadelle & les ports d'*Athènes*, ceux des *Propylées*, du *Temple de Minerve*, du *Temple d'Erechtée*, du *Théatre*, du *Gymnase*, du *Pirée*, de *Phalère*, pour *Sparte*, ceux du *Théatre*, du *Dromos*, du *Théatre de Délos*, d'un *Temple de Corinthe*, d'un *Temple à Pola en Istrie*, dédié à *Auguste*.

On rapportera les extraits des ouvrages de *Pausanias*, qui nous a donné des descriptions si magnifiques des édifices de la Grèce. Ce sont ces descriptions qui ont servi de guides dans la construction des Plans & de la Carte. Par-là le lecteur pourra suivre avec plus de facilité les recherches que l'on a faites, & admettre ou rejetter les conjectures de l'auteur, selon qu'elles lui paroîtront bien ou mal fondées. On trouvera de plus dans cette Partie l'histoire & les inscriptions des Monumens dont on donne les vûes, avec les passages des auteurs anciennes de ce pays, sur son état actuel, & sur la manière d'y voyager. On n'oubliera pas de relever les méprises des quatre voyageurs que j'ai cités. Enfin, cette première Partie de l'ouvrage sera précédée d'un Discours sur l'histoire de l'Architecture.

On rassemblera dans la seconde Partie les plans géométraux, les façades & les profils des édifices avec toutes leurs mesures. On ne les détaillera pas également, parce qu'il semble qu'il n'y a que deux raisons qui puissent rendre les détails nécessaires; la première, qu'ils soient assez beaux pour être imités par les Artistes; la second, qu'ils puissent servir à l'histoire de l'Art. Les membres d'Architecture qui auront rapport aux deux objets de curiosité ou d'utilité dont on vient de parler, seront développés en grand; les autres ne le seront pas avec la même étendue.

Afin de rendre cette partie plus intéressante, on y joindra les profils des colonnes Dorique antiques de l'église de S. *Pierre-aux-liens* à Rome, ceux des colonnes & de l'entablement du Théâtre de *Marcellus* dans la meme ville, & quelques parties des Temples de *Paestum* au Royaume de Naples. Ces monumens curieux, comparés avec les Ordres Grecs, prouveront d'une manière claire & décisive ce que l'Histoire ne nous apprend qu'en général sur le passage de l'Architecture Grecque en Italie.

Les Desseins des monumens avec leurs mesures seront rangés de suite, selon l'Ordre de leur antiquité dans chacune des classes suivantes; la prémière renfermera les Ordres Doriques, la seconde les Ordres Ioniques, & la dernière les Corinthiens.

C'est d'après ces précieux restes des édifices antiques élèves en différens temps que l'on tâchera, autant que les objets pourront le permettre, de tracer ou de faire reconnaître la suite des progrès de l'Architecture en Grèce. On verra les premiers Architectes Grecs faire leurs colonnes lisses, d'une proportion courte, sans base, les chapiteaux sans moulures & les entablemens fort lourds. On verra leurs successeurs donner plus de légèreté à leurs colonnes, les orner de cannelures, enrichir les chapiteaux de moulures, en ajoûter un plus grand nombre aux entablemens, enfin donner à leurs édifices la plus grande magnificence, en les embellisant d'ornemens & de figures.

C'est encore par le parallèle que les Architectes pourront faire des plus beaux monumens Grecs, dont cette partie contiendra les Desseins géométraux, avec ceux qui ont été le plus admirés chez les Romaines, qu'ils seront en état de se former une idée plus précise du goût de chacun de ces peuples, & de comparer leur connoissance en Architecture avec les nôtres, afin d'en tirer de nouvelles lumières sur cet Art. Car, quelques systêmes que l'on nous ait donnés sur les principes du beau en Architecture, on ne peut s'empêcher de reconnoître que ce n'est point dans la nature seule qu'il les faut chercher, mais dans ces monumens qui sont les fruits heureux d'un nombre infini de tentatives, & qui ont enfin obtenu le suffrage & l'éloge de tous les gens de goût. L'exemple des plus grands Architectes Italiens & François paroît prouver ce que l'on avance: on sçait assez que *Michel-Ange, Palladio, Vignole, Perrault,* ne se sont rendus si habiles & si célèbres que par une étude profonde des monumens antiques. La route qu'ils nous ont tracée paroît être la plus sûre pour parvenir à exceller dans la grande Architecture, c'est-à-dire, dans celle qui a pour objet les Temples, les Palais, les Places, les Théâtres, enfin tous ces monumens publics qui montrent aux étrangers la grandeur d'une nation, & font admirer à la postérité son goût & sa magnificence.

Il y a aura dans cette seconde Partie trente-deux Planches de différens détails, plans, coupes & profils des Monumens contenus dans la première. Toutes ces Planches auront onze pouces de haut sur dix-sept de large. Cette seconde partie sera précédée d'un Discours sur les principes de l'Architecture.

Tels sont les différens objets que l'on a en vûe en donnant au Public *les Ruines des plus beaux Monumens de la Grèce,* & l'ordre dans lequel on a dessein de les traiter: le projet est sans doute fort étendu, & l'auteur ne se dissimule pas tout ce qu'il exige pour être bien rempli; aussi n'entreprend-il cet ouvrage qu'après y avoir été encouragé par les conseils, il ose dire même, par les suffrages de sçavans illustres, & de personnes éclairées. Il sera tous ses efforts pour le rendre aussi intéressant qu'utile, & il assure qu'il a employé tout le temps & tous les soins nécessaires, pour mesurer & dessiner les monumens avec toute l'exactitude qui lui a été possible, ayant eu en cela toutes sortes de facilités par la protection des Ministres de Sa Majesté dans le Levant.

Il n'y a personne qui n'applaudisse à ce projet. Il doit être gouté, non-seulement des gens de Lettres & des sçavans, mais de tous les amateurs, de tous les connoisseurs, & de tous ceux dont l'ame n'est pas absolument assoupie dans d'épais organes. Quel charme, quelle volupté de voir, en quelque sorte, de ses propres yeux les deux plus fameuses villes de la Grèce, & de visiter ces Places, ces Théâtres, ces Portiques, si illustrés par les Orateurs, les Poëtes & les Philosophes!

Le papier sera du grand Colombier, & tout formera un volume *in folio* de la même grandeur que le superbe livre des *Ruines de Palmyre.* . . .

III. Preliminary draft of introduction for Ruins . . . at Spalatro

L. "Reasons and Motives for Undertaking the Voyage to Spalatro in Dalmatia" (Robert Adam, ERO, GD18/4953):

The Roman Nation which once shone so Conspicuous not only as a People, But in its particular Members, Has ever since attracted the attention of the whole World. There are very few who are not more knowing in their History than even in that of their own Country, and who have not conceived the highest Idea of their Grandeur and Magnificence. Of these we have now nothing left excepting the Remains of their Buildings. Is it then wonderful that we Should have the strongest inclination to see these Monuments of Roman Greatness! I must confess my own Desire was unbounded. For at the same time that I hoped to Satisfy my Curiosity, I doubted not, but I might be enabled to improve that Art which I had from My earlyest Days made Choice of as my Profession. I therefore resolved to Spend some Years at Rome and the other parts of Italy in the Study of these Buildings many of which had much exceeded my most Sanguine expectations. In remarking the manner of Construction and Disposition which the Ancients made use of, In taking accurate Drawings of their principal Ruins, and in making Myself as much Master of their proportions as I possibly cou'd.

The Publick Baths of which Two remain pretty entire at Rome, Viz. those of Diocletian and Carracalla Have been amongst the most extensive and Noble Buildings of the Ancients. By them these Emperors have shown Mankind that true Grandeur was only to be produced from Simplicity and largeness of Parts and that conveniency was not inconsistent with decoration. On them therefore I bent particularly my attention. And though any Accident shou'd for ever prevent me from publishing to the World my Drawings and Reflexions on that Subject, Yet I must own they contributed very much to the improvement of my Taste, and enlarged my Notions of Architecture whilst at the same time those of Diocletian afforded the first Hint about undertaking this Work which I now lay before the Publick.

The high opinion I had form'd of that Prince not only from his Baths at Rome But from the Accounts of his extraordinary expences bestowed on Building, at Nicomedia Milan Palmyra and many other places of his Empire, The Delicacy of his Taste which had often occasioned his pulling down Edifices he had executed, In order to rebuild them with Improvements, and that at immence charge Though in other Respects an Oconomical Manager of the Publick Money. These Circumstances together with what I had both heard and Read of a private Palace which that Emperor had built at Spalatro in Dalmatia convinced me that I might there find something worthy of Publick attention, and therefore I determined to lay before it the Draughts of a Palace once the Residence of so great a Prince. But what still further excited my curiosity was the Hopes of throwing some new Lights upon the private Buildings of the Ancients, A Subject which had hitherto been so Superficially handled that I doubted not It would render such an undertaking still more acceptable to the Publick. . . .

After Sailing six Days with unfavourable Winds we arrived at Pola in Istria about 50 Leagues distant from Venice. At this Place once a Colony of the Romans, there is still such Beautiful remains of their Architecture as wou'd certainly have induced me to spend some time in taking particular Drawings of them had I not heard that Messrs Stuart and Rivet two British Artists some few Years before had plan'd these Antiquity's. Their Characters for Knowledge and Exactness in these Matters determined me at once to drop the Prosecution of this Work which I doubted not when Published by them would afford general Satisfaction to the Publick. . . .

. . . And in this I have followed the Example of a Gentleman who has already given to the Publick Two most learned and perfect Works By which he has so deservedly acquired universal Approbation. To him Brittain in great measure owes that Rise of Taste and Love for Antique Architecture with which it is at present so happily Inspired And gives the Highest Encouragement for People of Genius to Search for and bring from Obscurity many valuable Monuments as yet unknown and to give just representations of those Remains which have hitherto been negligently or unskillfully represented. . . .

Besides the Ground Plan of the Palace I have given a Plan of the Town and its Environs, perspective views of the Town and of every part of the Ruin with Geo-metrical Elevations and Sections of its particular Buildings and General Elevations and Sections of the whole united together with their Measures and Proportions, As also the Detail of its Orders and Ornaments to a larger Scale. But as all these are more fully particularized in my Explanation of the Plates and the Materials of the different parts of the Work there mentioned I again refer my Reader to it and to the Plates themselves for more distinct Information, and shall only observe further that to make the whole more Compleat, I have from the Authority's of Ancient Authors and the general Maxims followed by the Ancients themselves in the Distribution of their Villas and private Buildings made out a Plan of the Palace in its perfect State which is referred to and described in the particular Discourse concerning the Restoration of Diocletians Palace. . . .

APPENDIX II

EXCERPTS FROM REVIEWS, CORRESPONDENCE, ETC., ON THE ARCHAEOLOGICAL PUBLICATIONS

Contents

Projects and publications of the Levant

1748 **ANTIQUITIES OF ATHENS**, Rome Proposal (Appendix I, entry A).

1751 **ANTIQUITIES OF ATHENS**, Venice Proposal (Appendix I, entry C).

1752 **MUSAEUM GRAECUM**

1. *JB*, VII, April 1752, pp. 454–455 (notice: two parts at two Guineas each: Part I, 23 plates of Athens; Part II, not yet published, 20 plates of Constantinople, Egypt, Asia Minor).

2. John Dalton, *Remarks on XII Historical Designs of Raphael and the Musaeum Graecum et Aegyptiacum*, London, 1752, pp. 13–14 (prospectus):

You justly observe, that our learned and ingenious Countrymen, as well as Foreigners, who have published their Travels into those celebrated Seats of Arts and Empire, how well soever they may have deserved of us in other Particulars, have sadly disappointed up by their Prints, which have misrepresented and disguised the noblest Remains of Antiquity. . . .

Now I am fully convinc'd that we shall not be led into any of these kinds of Mistakes by Mr *Dalton's Musaeum*. 'Tis certain, that he has had an Opportunity of making these Drawings on the Spot; and was engag'd to do it by a very sensible and worthy young Nobleman, the Lord Viscount Charlemont, who saw how imperfect all Books of Travels relating to those Prints had been, by the Want of accurate Drawings.

3. *Remarks on Prints . . . of the Present Inhabitants of Egypt*, London, 1781, pp. 8–9:

In the Year 1752, a short description, by way of letter, was published . . . in which an account is given, of the difficulty of making those sketches, with hopes of presenting them to the public. . . . The Editor, at that time, found himself much deceived in his expectatons, and was obliged to abandon all thoughts of any further publications, both on account of the great expence of the engravers, and other attending ones, as the whole cost in publishing those Views and Antiquities fell upon himself.

The great expectations formed of the Views and Antiquities of Athens, to be then engraved from the drawings of Messrs Stuart and Rivett, as also those of Palmyra and Balbec, put an entire stop to all further proceedings at that time, and since, he being very fortunately much better engaged under a most gracious protection.

1752   **ANTIQUITIES OF ATHENS** Athens Proposal (Appendix I, entry E.)

4. Thomas Hollis to John Ward, 25 December 1752 (BM, MS Add. 6210, fol. 101: cited in *Original Letters of Eminent Literary Men*, ed. Henry Ellis, London, 1843, p. 393):

More than once have I heard of Stuarts and Rivetts going on prosperously in Greece, and the last week their new Proposals were sent me by Mr Brittingham from Rome. These should certainly have been enclosed to you, had they not been effectively the same as the first, though somewhat more methodized, and that by this time they must be to be met with in England. Stuart has several times acknowledged to his friends here in Italy the many kind civilities and assistances received from Mr Dawkins. Really they deserve encouragement, and all those I meet, like to that gentleman, are disposed to give it.

5. *JB*, X, January–February 1753, pp. 165–172 (notice and French translation of proposal: Appendix I, entry G).

1753   **RUINS OF PALMYRA**

6. *JB*, VII, April 1752, pp. 453–454:

Deux voyageurs, qui ont fait le tour de la mer méditeranée en 1750. & en 1751., accompangés d'un dessinateur habile, ont recueilli dans leurs courses une grande quantité de figures d'antiquités, dont le Public profitera. Le premier recueil, qu'on lui promet consiste en plus de LX. planches en tailles douces. Elles représenteront les ruines de cette ville, dont l'histoire a si peu parlé, & qui dans ses débris conserve tant de restes de magnificence & de grandeur, je veux dire de Palmyre. Les desseins que j'ai vus sont d'une grande beauté, & comme on ne négligera rien dans le choix des graveurs, & dans l'éxécution de tout l'ouvrage, les souscripteurs n'auront pas lieu de regretter les trois guinées qu'on leur demande.

Ce sera encore un Ouvrage bien digne des plus belles Bibliothèques que celui que Mr. Dalton donne au public sous le titre de *Musaeum Graecum & Aegyptiacum* . . .

7. *JB*, XII, September–October 1753, pp. 3–41:

. . . ils ont enfin pris, à la manière de Desgodets, les dimensions des restes des anciens édifices de la Lydie, de la Ionie, & de la Carie. Ces matériaux pourroient servir à une histoire des progrès de l'Architecture depuis Pericles, jusqu'à Diocletien. Mais il faudroit y joindre les monumens, qui subsistent encore à Athènes & dans le territoire de l'Attique. Contens de satisfaire à cet égard leur curiosité particulière, nos voyageurs ont laissé à Mrs. Stewart & Revet le soin de satisfaire celle du public.

. . . Mr. Dawkins, content de travailler à l'instruction du Public, par les mesures qu'il a prises lui-même sur les lieux des divers morceaux représentés dans ces planches, a cédé à Mr. Wood le soin & le profit de la publication.

. . . Ce Temple [du Soleil] n'est pas plus remarquable par sa grandeur & par sa magnificence que par ses singularités. Les connoisseurs d'architecture sauront les discerner, & Mr. Wood leur en laisse le soin. On ne peut ce semble que regarder comme un défaut, les avances dont le fût des colonnes est interrompu au tiers de leur hauteur . . .

L'Architecture & la sculpture se sont en général suivies: mais le sculpture est arrivée plûtôt à sa perfection, & en est plus vite déchue.

8. *LG*, 13 November 1753 (advertisement).

9. *LG*, 20 November 1753 (notice of publication).

10. *LM*, XXII, November 1753, p. 535 (notice).

11. *GM*, XXIII, November 1753, p. 542 (notice).

12. *MR*, IX, December 1753, pp. 439–443 (review):

. . . this beautiful and elegant work, . . . must give the highest entertainment to all who are lovers of architecture and sculpture . . .

13. *JB*, XII, November–December 1753, p. 427 (notice of publication of French translation).

14. H. Walpole to R. Bentley, 19 December 1753 (*Letters of Horace Walpole*, ed. Toynbee, Oxford, 1903–1905, III, p. 202):

. . . Palmyra is come forth, and is a noble book; the prints finely engraved, and an admirable dissertation before it. My wonder is much abated: the Palmyrene empire which I had figured, shrunk to a small trading city with some magnificent public buildings out of proportion to the dignity of the place.

15. *Adventurer*, 22 January 1754 (ed. Hawkesworth, new ed., III, 1794, pp. 335–336):

The supreme excellence of the ancient ARCHITECTURE . . . has never once been called in question, and because it is abundantly testified by the awful ruins of amphitheatres, acqueducts, arches, and columns, that are the daily objects of veneration, though not of imitation. This art, it is observable, has never been improved in later ages in one single instance; but every just and legitimate edifice is still formed according to the five old established orders, to which human wit had never been able to add a sixth of equal symmetry and strength.

Such, therefore, are the triumphs of the ANCIENTS, especially the GREEKS, over the MODERNS. They may, perhaps, be not unjustly ascribed to a genial climate, that gave such a happy temperment of body as was most proper to produce fine sensations; to a language most harmonious, copious, and forcible. . . .

16. *Connoisseur*, 7 February 1754, p. 13:

A correspondent desires to know, whether I was of that party, that lately took a survey of *Palmyra in the Desart*; another, if I have traversed the *Holy Land*, or visited *Mount Calvary*. I shall not speak too proudly of my travels: but as my predecessor the SPECTATOR has recommended himself by having made a trip to *Grand Cairo* to take measure of a pyramid, I assure my reader, that I have climbed *Mount Vesuvio* in the midst of it's eruptions, and dug some time underground in the ruins of *Herculaneum*.

17. *Adventurer*, 5 March 1754 (ed. Hawkesworth, new ed., III, 1794, pp. 447–448):

. . . the Greek and Roman architecture are discarded for the novelties of China; the RUINS OF PALMYRA, and the copies of the capital pictures of CORREGIO, are neglected for gothic designs, and burlesque political prints . . .

Perhaps it may be thought, that if this be, indeed, the state of learning and taste, an attempt to improve it by a private hand is romantic, and the hope of success chimerical: but to this I am not solicitous to give other answer, than that such an attempt is consistent with the character in which this paper is written; and that the ADVENTURER can assert, upon classical authority, that in brave attempts it is glorious even to fail.

18. *AL*, 6 March 1754, I, pp. 183–193 (review):

On ne trouve plus, Monsieur, que des fragmens épars de l'Architecture ancienne:

restes précieux qui peuvent encore diriger le goût de nos Artistes. Des descriptions faites avec soin de ces monumens célèbres sont très-propres à satisfaire la curiosité du Public, & à contribuer aux progrès de l'Art.

. . . Le tout est rendu avec une précision & une entente qui sont un honneur infini aux Auteurs de ce superbe Recueil.

Pour donner à ces desseins généraux plus d'agrément, on a ajouté dans plusieurs Planches des frontons, qu'on suppose avoir été élevés lors de la perfection de ces édifices, aussi-bien que d'autres parties entières, que les fragmens qui restent annoncent y avoir été. Ces additions ont déja fait croire & dire à plusieurs personnes que le Peristyle du Louvre, bâti par *Claude Perrault*, avoit été fait sur le modèle de ces ruines; & l'on se fonde encore sur ce que l'ordre de ce Temple est Corinthien, & que les niches & les croisées, couronnées de petits frontons, on beaucoup de ressemblance avec le Peristyle. Mais ne pourroit-on pas dire, au contraire, que ce sont les beautés du Peristyle dans son état actuel, qui ont donné l'idée de completter dans ce Recueil ces fameuses ruines? Quoi qu'il en soit, cette imitation prétendu de la part de *Perrault*, quand elle seroit réelle, ne pourroit que lui faire honneur. Plût à Dieu que nos Artistes méritassent des reproches de cette espèce! Nous n'aurions pas tant d'édifices d'une ordonnance si négligée, & d'une décoration, pour la plûpart, si triviale. . . .

Cet ouvrage intéresse les amateurs de l'Antiquité & tous les Artistes. On ne sauroit trop recommander à ces derniers l'étude de ce Recueil & l'examen des Desseins, dont la plûpart des profils sont excellens, les ornemens d'un bon choix & distribués avec art, les formes belles en général, & toutes tracées avec une exactitude qui mérite les plus grands éloges.

Il n'y a personne, pour peu qu'il ait d'ame & de goût, qui ne se sente émû à l'aspect de ces merveilles de l'Antiquité, & qui ne soit pénétré d'estime & de reconnoissance pour d'illustres Voyageurs, qui, conduits par le seul amour des Arts & du bien public, ont volontairement consacré leur loisir, leurs veilles, leur santé, leurs richesses, à nous procurer tant de chefs-d'oeuvres, & à les transmettre à la Postérité. M. *Dawkins* a droit sur-toit à la gratitude de notre âge & des siècles à venir. Ce généreux Anglois ne s'est pas borné à vouloir que tout fût fait avec la plus grande exactitude à prendre lui-même presque toutes les mesures qu'on trouve dans cet ouvrage: sensible au seul intérêt des Arts & de leur avancement, il a abandonné à M. *Wood* tout le profit qui pourra revenir de cette entreprise.

19. *World*, 14 March 1754, pp. 377–383:

Yet many there are, and men of taste too, as the phrase goes, who through a shameful neglect of their MINDS, have little or no relish of the fine arts: and I doubt whether, in our most splendid assemblies, the ROYAL GAME OF GOOSE would not have as many eyes fixed upon it, as the lately published curiosity of the ruins of PALMYRA. I mention this work not only to inform such of your readers, as do not labour under a total loss of appetite for liberal amusements, what a sumptuous entertainment they may sit down to, but also to give it as a signal instance, how agreeably men of ingenious talents, ample fortune, and great leisure, may amuse themselves, and, laudably employing their leisure-time, do honour to their country.

20. *JS*, April 1754, pp. 391–411 (review: included in J. J. Barthélemy, *Oeuvres diverses*, Paris, 1798, I, pp. 185–201):

Nous recueillons les premiers fruits d'une expédition littéraire, fait par une société libre, éclairée, dont les opérations, asservies à un plan régulier, ne pouvaient être, ni précipitées, ni retardées par des ordres supérieurs ou par des vues d'intérêt, et qui ne doit qu'à elle-même gloire d'avoir exécuté une grande entreprise.

. . . Instruits des avantages que l'on a retirés du livre de M. Desgodets sur les édifices de l'ancienne Rome, ils dirigeaient souvent leur attention vers ces monuments qui embellissaient autrefois la plupart des villes de l'Orient, et dont, en plusieurs endroits, il ne reste que des débris informes, qu'il fallait quelquefois arracher des entrailles de la terre. Dans ces ruines qui, malgré les ravages du temps et des hommes, conservent encore l'empreinte du goût particulier à chaque siècle, ils étudiaient l'origine et les progrès de l'architecture; et c'est sur des pièces si justificatives qu'ils se trouvent en état de donner l'histoire de ce bel art, et sur-tout des changements qu'il a éprouvés depuis le siècle de Périclès jusqu'à celui de Dioclétian.

Après les détails ou nous sommes entrés, il est inutile d'avertir qu'en publiant ce livre, on n'a rien oublié pour que la beauté du papier et l'élégance des graveurs répondissent à la grandeur d'une entreprise qui honore la nation anglaise, et qui doit intéresser toutes les autres.

21. *BSBA*, I, Part 1, January–March 1754, p. 234 (notice):

La grande quantité d'Inscriptions Grecques & Palmyriennes, qui s'y trouvent copiées avec la derniére exactitude, est digne entre autres choses d'exciter l'admiration des curieux.

22. *GGA*, 29 August 1754, Part 2, pp. 897–903 (review):

. . . wir glauben der gelehrten Welt dadurch eine wahre Freude zu machen, wann wir melden, dasz sie sich mit der Zeit noch mehrere andere dergleichen sonderbare und merkwurdige Nachrichten von der Neubegierde dieser Reisenden zu versprochen habe. . . .

. . . Vermuthlich was es der Reichthum, welcher die Einwohner wollüstig und zugleich faul und weiblich gemacht hat. Weswegen sich nachher um so weniger zu verwundern ist, dasz nach dem Verlust ihrer Freyheit eine so prächtige, aber an einer unfruchtbaren Gegend gelegne Stadt so schleunig wiederum in ihr erstes Richts hat verfallen können.

23. *MF*, September 1754, pp. 18–45 (review).

24. C. Natoire to A. F. P. Marigny, 24 December 1754 (*CD*, XI, pp. 62–63):

. . . Il m'a fait, ses jours passés, un présent pour l'Académie d'un beaux livre que vous connoissés san doutte, qui et *les Ruines de Palmyre*, fait en Engleterre; il contoit en faire présent au Pape; mais S. S. l'avoit reçu quelques jours auparavent par l'éditeur. Cela a fait beaucoup de plaisir á nos architectts.

25. P. Patte, *Discours sur l'architecture*, Paris, 1754, pp. 34–35:

On mettra sous les yeux [in order to learn architecture] les desseins des plus beaux Edifices de la Gréce & de l'Italie qui subsistent encore en entier ou en partie; & à leur défaut les Edifices antiques de Degodets, les ruines de Palmire, l'Architecture historique de Wischer, le Vitruve de Perrault, les magnifiques compositions du célébre Piranesi. Rien n'est plus propre à donner une grande idée de la haute maniére de l'Architecture antique, & à former ce discernement sûr, qui fait reconnoître & saisir d'abord le beau sous quelque forme qu'il se présente, surtout lorsque'un Maître habile sert d'interprête à ces bâtimens, & n'en laisse passer aucun sans en motiver les perfections & même les défauts qui peuvent quelquefois s'y rencontrer.

26. *NAG*, March 1756, pp. 173–177 (review).

27. *NAE*, June 1756, pp. 300–307 (review):

Magnum, spectandumque imprimis opus, ingenti volumine codicis speciosi, picturae linearis beneficio, nitidissime curatis adumbranda rerum specie picturae linearis ex aere tabulis, quae commentario illustravit longae, ac dissicilimae, discriminisque plenae peregrinationis comes, Rupertus Gevoldus nomine, (*Mr. Wood*) laeti studiis monumentorum veterum lubentesque videmus. Vix illud tale ac tantum sidem erat inventurum, nisi olim affirmatum aliorum peregrinatium diversis testimoniis, nunc magno requisitum, exploratum, excussumque animo, sic minutim descriptum summa industria, proponeretur, ut iam amplius dubitandi de summo ac paene incredibili Palmyrae vel excisae splendore nullus sit locus futurus. . . .

. . . Haec superiora nos optimo quidem consilio, quatenus eorum aliqua suspensos attinere studiosorum hominum animos, in opere magno & ad summam probando, posse putabamus, in litteras referenda habuimus. Reliqua omnia, nostro certe animo, praeclara ibi, ut memoravimus, ac merita laude celebranda sunt.

28. Robert Adam to James Adam, 1 November 1757 (ERO, GD18/4843):

. . . I am not for praising the Taste of W.ds work, the greatest connoisseurs here, are of my own private opinion that Taste & Truth, or as W. terms it, Accuracy, are not the Characteristicks or Qualifications of these Works. They are as hard as Iron, & as false as Hell; You can likewise consider that as Stuarts Work will be published & that we all know How much the very fame of it has blasted the Reputation of these Works of P———a & B———k, may it not be Reckon'd want of taste, or Rather Envy & Jealousy not to say something about them, & to talk so highly of Inferiour Works ——— ——— as to the time My Work took it

Stands thus, W left Venice the 11th July & arrived at Spalatro the 22d of July. The 28th of August left Spalatro & the 11th of September arrived at Venice So that you can see we were just 5 Weeks at Spalatro—& that Time 4 people were Constantly at Work which is equal to 20 Weeks of one person. Mr W—d was but 15 days at Palmyra & had but one Man to Work for him, judge of the Accuracy of such a Work.

1755   **ANTIQUITIES OF ATHENS,** London Proposal (Appendix I, entry J).

1756   **RUINES . . . DE LA GRÈCE,** Proposal (Appendix I, entry K).

29. J. J. Barthélemy to A. C. P. Caylus, 10 December 1755 (Barthélemy, *Voyage en Italie*, Paris, an X [1801], pp. 49–50):

Je vous fais mon compliment sur l'ouvrage de M. Leroi; je désire comme vous qu'il paroisse; mais je souhaiterois que vous laissassiez passer d'abord celui des Anglais. Ne seroit-il pas possible que plusieurs personnes eussent mieux vu qu'une seule? Ces Anglais ne sont pas ceux de Palmyre: c'est une autre troupe qui a demeuré longtemps à Athènes, et dont l'ouvrage, dit-on, ne tardera pas à paroître: j'en ai entendu dire beaucoup de bien à des gens indifférens. Si par hasard il valoit mieux que celui de M. Leroi, cette nation avantageuse triompheroit. Vous connoissez mieux que moi la force de l'objection, et je la soumets à votre avis.

30. *JE,* 15 April 1756, pp. 54–57 (announcement of prospectus).

31. *MF,* April 1756, pp. 76–77 (summary of Appendix I, entry K).

32. *NAG,* August 1759, pp. 565–573:

. . . Solche Vorgänger [Wood, Dawkins, Norden] nun reizeten den Hrn. le Roy, im 1753sten Jahre, da er sich zu Rom befand, nach Greichenland zu gehen, um sich eine gröszere Kenntnisz der alten Baukunst zu erwerben; und einen Theil der groszen Absichten zu erfüllen, die seine Nation im vorigen Jahrhunderte gefasset hatte.

. . . Alles ist prächtig, und im gröszten Formate gedruckt und gestochen.

33. Bareau de Chefdeville to W. Chambers, 5 May 1757 (RIBA Library):

. . . Le Roy n'a pas encore mis aujour[d'hui] son livre, evidamadt que dans quatre mois il esperoit le faire paroitre, il vaut la paine d'etre achepté. je lui ai dit que je souscrivoit pour deux la Souscription ende 94th ainsy cesera 108th Les deux il m'a dit que l'avoit eu plusiers souscription pour londe. je ne lui pas rendre comte que c'etoit pour vous les deux exemplaire[s] que je lui ai demandé [word illegible] Le livre de LeRoy est bien vendue et bien ecrit je mis certain qui l'eut vou[s] vena un grand debit.

1757   **RUINS OF BALBEC**

34. *LM,* XXVI, April 1757, pp. 158–159 (excerpt from *Balbec*).

H

35. *LM*, XXVI, April 1757, p. 207 (notice).

36. *GM*, XXVII, May 1757, p. 243 (notice).

37. *UM*, XXI, July 1757, pp. 28–32 (extract from *Balbec*: reprinted in *Lloyd's Evening Post*, 12–15 August 1757, p. 87; 15–17 August 1757, pp. 93–94).

38. *CR*, IV, July 1757, pp. 46–51 (review):
This *classical* part of their travels, with the illustration of *antient fable*, will be a valuable acquisition to the learned world . . . the ruins of Balbec will afford the lover of art and *virtù* the highest satisfaction, as they will exhibit to him the finest remains of antient architecture perhaps now in the world. . . . Mr. Wood . . . informs us, that Mr. Dawkins, with the same generous spirit which had so indefatigably surmounted the various obstacles of their voyage, continued, during Mr. Wood's unavoidable absence, to protect the fruits of those labours which he had so chearfully shared; and that he not only attended to the accuracy of the work, by having finished drawings made under his own eye by their draughtsman, from the sketches and measures he had taken on the spot, but had the engravings so far advanced as to be now ready for the public under their joint inspection.

39. *NAG*, August 1757, pp. 605–613 (review).

40. *JB*, XXIV, November–December 1757, pp. 293–309 (review):
. . . la Grand-Bretagne est particulierement redevable du rang qu'elle tient dans le monde Litéraire, aux Savans qui ont donné au public, les Ruines de Palmyre & de Balbec. Leurs travaux pénibles & les dangers auxquels ils se sont exposés dans la recherche de ces restes inestimables de l'Antiquité, suffiroient pour nous engager à les estimer & à les admirer. . . . on considere la valeur du trésor qu'ils ont découvert, l'exactitude extraordinaire des desseins, l'élegance des planches, l'explication qu'ils en donnent & les Observations judicieuses de ses Voyageurs infatigables. . . .

41. *MR*, XVIII, January 1758, pp. 59–66 (review: section cited in John Nichols, *Literary Anecdotes* . . . , London, 1817–1858, III, p. 85):
Of all the antiquities that have been communicated to the world; of all the remains of antient monuments brought from the East, none can be compared with the ruins of Palmyra, and of Balbec; not only on account of their stupendous mangificence, but for the extraordinary diligence of those gentlemen who have favoured the public with this view of them, and the accuracy, and elegance of the designs. We are authorized in saying this much, by the unanimous consent of all the Literati in Europe. But it is with particular pleasure we observe such a Work as this produced at a time when war seemed to have engrossed the attention of mankind. The drawn sword has not yet frightened the Muses from their seat: they have more dangerous enemies in the Chinese and Goths, than in the sons of Mars. Such specimens of architecture as have already been communicated to the public, by the learned and ingenious Editor of the Ruins of Balbec, with others which are

expected of Athens, &c. will, we hope, improve the taste of our countrymen, and expell the littleness and ugliness of the Chinese, and the barbarity of the Goths, that we may see no more useless and expensive trifles; no more dungeons instead of summer-houses.

42. H. Walpole to H. Mann, 9 February 1758 (*Horace Walpole's Correspondence*, New Haven, 1960, XXI, Part 5, p. 173):
. . . The *Palmyra* and *Balbec* are noble works to be undertaken and executed by private men. . . .

43. *JE*, 1 February 1758, I, Part 3, p. 146 (notice).

44. *JE*, 15 May 1758, IV, Part 1, pp. 110–119 (review):
De tous les monumens antiques qui nous restent, il n'en est peut-être point de plus dignes de notre admiration que les ruines de Palmyre & de Balbec. Malgré les outrages du tems à qui tout cede, la magnificence & la grandeur percent encore à travers ces restes de l'antiquité, & inspirent je ne sçai quel respect pour la mémoire de ceux à qui l'on en est redevable. . . .

L'Editeur des ruines de Balbec a déja donné au public plusieurs modeles d'Architecture si parfaits, qu'on espere qu'ils detruiront le mauvais goût, qui ne craint pas de substituer la petitesse des Chinois & la barbarie des Goths à la grandeur & à la magnificence des anciens Romains.

. . . Nous attendons avec impatience de la même main [Wood's] les ruines d'Athenes, dont nous ne manquerons pas de parler dans le tems.

45. *AL*, 8 November 1758, VII, pp. 3–15 (review):
. . . [les bâtiments de l'antiquité] sont nos modèles sans doute, mais pour être leurs imitateurs, non leurs plagiaires; c'est l'esprit de leurs ouvrages & de leurs leçons qu'il faut saisir. Les préceptes de l'Architecture sont-ils donc devenus de nos jours de nature à ne pouvoir être suivis? Et ne semble-t-il pas qu'on prenne plaisir à substituer le désordre dans nos bâtimens à ce qu'on appelle les Ordres d'Architecture proprement dits? . . . ces . . . édifices semblent être érigés pour prouver à la multitude que les beautés de l'Architecture sont arbitraires . . . Je crains que le Recueil . . . qui fait véritablement honneur aux Anglois, ne produise encore à l'avenir des abus en Architecture, dignes des Goths. . . . Je crains enfin que cet ouvrage, plein de beautés sans nombre, mais contrebalancé par des parties de détail d'un moindre prix, ne serve d'autorité aux hommes superficiels. Que de graces à leur rendre, au contraire, s'ils vouloient, avec discernement, faire usage de la belle disposition des Portiques de ce Recueil, des Colonnades, des Croisées, des Frises, répandus dans les Planches 25, 26, 30, 31, 32, & 41! Mais qui nous répondra que, par une imitation condamnable, ils n'iront pas préférer la plûpart des niches, des petits colonnes, des tabernacles, des frontons sur l'angle, des corniches & des appuis suspendus, des compartimens & des ornemens trop surchargés, des entablemens qu'on remarque dans les Planches 4, 6, 7, 16, 17, 18, 29, 44 & 46 de *Balbec*, aussi, bien que dans les

Planches 11, 17, 19, 22, 47 & 50 de *Palmyre*, les uns & les autres monumens de l'enfance de l'Art plutôt que sa perfection?

46. *NAE*, October 1759, pp. 577–590 (review):

In iis, quae nuper de hodierna conditione ruinarum Palmyrae dicebamus, iter ab Angli quibusdam litterarum studiosis in Palaestinam susceptum diligentius persequebamur, eosque etiam enarrationis de Balbeci ruderibus edendae spem secisse, Lectoribus nostris affirmabamus. Quam ab ipsis nunc esse praestitam fidem, plane nulli dubitamus quin antiquitatis omnis et architecturae inprimis studiosi sint cum gaudio atque delectatione accepturi, suoque suffragio studium Anglorum de literis et artibus bene merendi approbaturi, qui pede coepere pergentium bonarum artium pomeria proferre. Haec altera, de qua nunc exponemus, itinerarii pars ab illis profecti, non solum illi superiori, neque gravitate rerum, neque operis splendore, neque diligentia conscriptionis, neque copiis doctrinae, quicquam concedit: sed etiam tam utilis, tam iucundi, eiusdemque tam nobilis et magni incepti continuationem pollicetur. . . .

Brevitas instituti nostri non patitur, ut de imaginibus aere excusis multum praedicemus, aut maiestatem et artificia architecturae, quae in iis ab intelligentibus animadverti facile possint, verbis extollamus. Quare eius artis amatores ad ipsum opus ablegamus, hoc ipsis adfirmantes, in eo sex quinquaginta imagines caelo ductas reperturos eos esse, sed plenas illas architecturae miraculis, si quidem testimonio tam prudentum, tam doctorum tam denique candidorum Virorum, atque sunt Wodius et Dawkinsius, fides haberi potest. Et potest certe.

47. *BSW*, V, 1759, pp. 190–191 (review).

48. *The Ruins of Athens*, ed. Sayer, 1759, Preface (see entry 67 below).

49. *JS*, June 1760, pp. 303–328 (review: reprinted in J. J. Barthélemy, *Oeuvres diverses*, Paris, 1798, I, pp. 202–223):

. . . cet auteur . . . ne cherche point à étaler le faste de l'érudition, n'epuise jamais l'art frivole et fastidieux des conjectures, et se contente de montrer une supériorité de connaissance et de raison; aussi nous n'hésitons pas à regarder le discours qu'il a placé à la tête des *Ruines de Palmyre*, et celui dont nous rendons compte aujourd'hui, comme deux modèles en matière de critique.

50. James Adam to Betty Adam, 15 July 1760 (ERO, GD18/4864):

Clerisseau had some time ago a letter from Mariette at Paris, about some Antiquities &ca. he concludes by desiring to be informed when his friends work of Spalatro will be finish'd & hopes there will be a French translation of it. as the expectations of the learn'd there are great, he is persuaded Mr. Wood had no reason to regret his having translated his Palmyra & Balbec into their language.

51. H. Walpole, *Anecdotes of Painting*, Strawberry Hill, 1762, pp. xiii–xiv:

But of all the works that distinguish this age, none perhaps excel those beautiful

editions of Balbec and Palmyra—not published at the command of a Louis quat-
orze, or at the expence of a cardinal nephew, but undertaken by private curiosity
and good sense, and trusted to the taste of a polished nation. When I endeavour to
do justice to the editions of Palmyra and Balbec, I would not confine the encom-
ium to the sculptures; the books have far higher merit. The modest descriptions
prefixed are standards of writing: The exact measure of what should and should
not be said, and of what was necessary to be known, was never comprehended in
more clear diction, or more elegant stile. The pomp of the buildings has not a
nobler air than the simplicity of the narration . . .

52. *Ruins . . . at Spalatro*, London, 1764, Preface, p. 4:
    Encouraged by the favorable reception which has been given of late to works of
this kind, particularly to the Ruins of Palmyra and Balbec, I now present the fruits
of my labor to the public. I am far from comparing my undertaking with that of
Messieurs Dawkins, Bouverie, and Wood, one of the most splendid and liberal
that was ever attempted by private persons, I was not, like those gentlemen,
obliged to traverse desarts, or to expose myself to the insults of barbarians, nor can
the remains of a single Palace vie with those surprizing and almost unknown monuments of sequestered grandeur which they have brought to light . . .

53. P. Patte, *Mémoires sur les objets les plus importans de l'Architecture*, Paris, 1769, p.
81 (cited in M. Mathieu, *Pierre Patte*, Paris, 1940, p. 112):
    Dans les ruines de la Grece, il n'y a pas un profil, ni un détail intéressant d'Archi-
tecture dont on puisse se promettre de faire usage avec succès en exécution; mais
dans celles du temple de Balbec et du palais du Soleil à Palmyre, on remarque par
endroits des ordonnances d'Architecture, des profils, des détails d'ornemens d'un
goût exquis, & dont avec discernement il seroit possible de faire des choix très-
avantageux.

54. H. Walpole, Epitaph for Wood (David Lysons, *The Environs of London*,
London, 1792–1796, I, p. 421):
    . . . The beautiful editions of Balbec and Palmyra, illustrated by the classic pen of
Robert Wood, supply a nobler and more lasting monument, and will survive
those august remains.

55. E. Gibbon, *Decline and Fall of the Roman Empire*, ed. J. B. Bury, New York,
1946 (1st ed. 1776–1788), I, p. 240, note 23:
    . . . Our curiosity has . . . been gratified in a . . . splendid manner by Messieurs
Wood and Dawkins.

56. Quatremère de Quincy, *Rapport . . . an II*, Paris, 1793, p. 65:
    Du temps de Soufflot, les ruines de Palmire & de Baalbeck étoient en vogue.
Les voyageurs Anglais venoient de publier leur bel ouvrage sur ces restes mémor-
ables, monumens du plus grand luxe auquel soit parvenu le Corinthien. Soufflot
tendit toutes ses cordes sur ce ton; il chercha la plus grande richesse: mais il prit

souvent le change, sa richesse devint superfluité & bientôt mesquinerie. Il ne fut pas
bien servi non plus par ceux qui lui brodoient son monument. Choix commun
d'ornemens en quelques parties, exécution précieuse, mais aride & maigre, mauv-
aise entente dans la distribution des masses & des détails: bref, l'effet ne répondit
pas à son attente.

1758   RUINES ... DE LA GRÈCE

57. P. J. Mariette to J. J. Barthélemy, 7 August 1758 (*PV*, VI, pp. 329–330):
L'Académie a reconnu dans les études qu'il a fait de ces monuments beaucoup
d'intelligence et de soin, et après en avoir conféré, elle est convenue de les examiner;
l'Académie luy a marqué toute la satisfaction que cet ouvrage méritte.

58. *Correspondance littéraire*, August 1758, p. 27 (review):
Les Ruines des plus beaux monumens de la Grèce viennent d'être achevées. Cet
ouvrage de M. LeRoy, entrepris sur modèle des *Ruines de Palmyre*, publiées en
Angleterre, avait été proposé par souscription en 1756. . . . Au jugement de tout le
monde, ce magnifique ouvrage est très-supérieur à tout ce que les Anglais ont
publié en ce genre.

59. *JE*, 1 October 1758, pp. 142–143 (notice and description).

60. *PV*, VI, 13 November 1758, pp. 334–335:
M. *Blondel* a lu à l'Académie son sentiment sur le livre de M. LeRoy intitulé
Les ruines de la Grèce, etc., dont la Compagnie l'avait chargé. La Compagnie a été
très satisfaite du livre et de l'éloge que M. *Blondel* en a fait; elle a même résolu d'en
faire la lecture dans ses conférences particulières.

61. *PV*, VI, 20 November 1758, pp. 335–336:
L'extrait que M. *Blondel* a fait du livre de M. Le Roy sur les ruines de la Grèce
ayant déterminé la Compagnie à donner son approbation à ce livre, et la lecture
que les architectes de l'Académie ont fait du même livre, tant dans les assemblées
ordinaires qu'en leur particulier, les ayant convaincu de l'étendue des connoissances de l'auteur et combien ses recherches laborieuses sur les ruines des édifices
les plus anciens et sur les lieux mêmes peuvent êtres utiles au progrès de l'architecture, l'Académie, pour donner à M. LeRoy des preuves de l'estime qu'elle fait de
son ouvrage, de son zèle et de ses talens, a cru devoir saisir l'occasion de la vacance
d'une place qui n'a point été rempli dans la seconde classe . . .

62. A. F. P. Marigny to J. Gabriel, 23 November 1758 (*PV*, VI, pp. 336–337):
J'ai lu, Monsieur, avec satisfaction la délibération de l'Académie du 20 de ce
mois au sujet du livre de M. Le Roy sur les ruines de la Grèce, et j'approuve avec
grand plaisir le désir qu'elle témoigne de s'associer un sujet qui, par l'étendu de ses
connoissances et par des recherches aussi curieuses que laborieuses, s'est rendu utile
aux arts et a là gloire de la nation. . . .

63. *JS*, November 1758, pp. 213–234; December 1758, pp. 141–158; pp. 252–267 (review):

. . . M. LeRoy a consulté les anciens Auteurs pour rapprocher ces ruines des époques de leurs Fondateurs; il a raisonné en Architecte, pour rendre utiles les recherches qu'il a faites dans le cours de son voyage.

Le voyage de M. LeRoy a été fait dans d'autres vües. C'est un Artiste qui a interrogé la Grèce expirante, qui l'a entendue donner ses dernières leçons sur l'Architecture, & qui nous rend aujourd'hui ces instructions, afin de dédommager notre siècle & la postérité des ravages qu'a causés la Barbarie dans tout l'ancien domaine des Grecs.

Ces Ordres ont tellement fixé les inclinations de tous les peuples cultivés, qu'ils peuvent être mis au rang des principes & des loix de l'Architecture. On sait quelles furent leurs proportions chez les Grecs: on tâche de les suivre, on les varie quelque-fois: la difficulté est de saisir ce qu'il y a de plus beau, de plus natural, de plus satis-faisant à l'oeil, de mieux approprié aux desseins de construction qu'on a dû se proposer. . . . Si nous étions plus Connoisseurs en Architecture, notre suffrage seroit d'un plus grand poids: c'est aux Maîtres de l'Art qu'il convient de prononcer ici en dernier ressort; mais pour ce jugement, il faudroit allier les lumières de la Littérature aux talents de l'Architecte. Il faudroit être Pline & Vitruve.

64. *AL*, 8 November 1758, VII, pp. 100–124 (review):

. . . Vous serez étonné, Monsieur, du courage, de la constance & des lumières qu'il a fallu à cet Architecte, habile dans son art & sçavant dans l'Antiquité, pour entreprendre seul le voyage pénible & dangereux de la Grèce, pour y dessiner les monumens dans les aspects les plus flatteurs, pour en lever exactement les plans, enfin, pour faire les recherches les plus profondes sur leur histoire, sur les particul-arités de leur Architecture, sur l'origine, les progrès & la nature des principes de son Art; car ne croyez pas que ce ne soit ici qu'un Recueil d'estampes; c'est un ouvrage trés-sçavant, très-méthodique & très-bien écrit sur plusieurs villes de la Grèce, sur les monumens qu'elles renferment, sur les mesures des Grecs, sur les différens Ordres de l'Architecture.

. . . Ainsi vous trouverez dans ce Recueil, Monsieur, non-seulement autant d'intérêt & d'exactitude que dans les *Ruines de Palmyre & de Balbec* . . . mais encore plus de sçavoir, de goût, d'ordre & de clarté. . . . Si l'auteur met sous les yeux des exemples qui ne sont plus d'usage aujourd'hui parmi les Artistes célèbres, c'est pour montrer l'origine de l'art, le gout des Architectes de la Grèce, & pour avoir lieu de faire des Dissertations sçavantes, capables d'empêcher le vulgaire de tomber dans une imitation servile. . . .

65. *MF*, January 1759, pp. 128–133; February 1759, pp. 105–111; February 1759 (suppl.), pp. 106–115 (review).

66. P. J. Mariette to G. G. Bottari, 10 February 1759 (Bottari, *Raccolta di lettere* . . . , Milan, 1822–1825, IV, p. 340):

. . . Io ho gusto, che alla prima occhiata, che avete data al libro delle *Antichità della Grecia*, sia stata favorevole a quest'opera. Spero, che ne farete anche più contento, quando l'avrete letta, perchè invero questo libro è scritto sensatamente, e contiene ecellenti note. . . .

67. *The Ruins of Athens*, ed. Sayer, 1759, Preface:

The great Ideas formed from consulting ancient Authors in their Descriptions of the famous Edifices in *Greece*, and the little Improvement or Certainty to be obtained of their real Excellence, from consulting modern Travellers, was the Motive and no doubt a very proper one, which induced Mons. *LeRoy*, a *Frenchman*, to visit the once so famed City of ATHENS: Who, there assisted by Royal Munificence and every other Requisite which could aid his own great Genius, has removed the Fable of Antiquity; and, by Representation, not only given us the present Situation of the Remains of those valuable Monuments, but, likewise, from his painful Researches into the various and just Proportions, filled our Imaginations with their former Beauty and Magnificence; and, at the same Time, by his Rules and Observations, given us many Lessons for easy and perfect Imitation.

And though we gladly acknowledge the Benefits received from Mess. *Wood* and *Dawkins*, yet we cannot but lament that their elegant Designs are without such Observations as must occur in those Treasures of Antiquity, which might improve or assist the best Architects of our Time . . .

. . . the supplying of . . . [the loss of an original & accurate version of Vitruvius] . . . as also an Attempt to restore Architecture to its ancient Dignity, are intended by the ensuing Work. A Work it is hoped, executed in such a Manner (no Inquiry, Labour or Expence having been spared) as to adorn the Libraries of the Learned and Curious; and, at the same Time, capable of aiding the Student, and assisting the Master, even to acquire in that Science what may be termed the Sublime.

68. *CR*, VIII, July 1759, pp. 70–82 (review: Sayer ed.):

The ruins before us must be generally admired as long as mankind retains a taste for magnificence, order, and regularity in building. They have this advantage over the ruins of the famous Palmyra, that they are the precepts of Vitruvius reduced into practice; precepts that are founded upon eternal laws, and coeval and coexisting with the ideas of beauty itself.

. . . this work may be justly considered as an attempt to restore architecture to its antient dignity; and of enabling the beholder and reader to attain to the correct sublime in that noble art, after its having been so long mistaken.

After all, we have certain reasons for declaring, that *LeRoy*'s plans are far from being correct; that his imagination in some places has run riot; that, in others, his drawings are faulty, his proportions false; and that the public will do well to suspend their opinion of this work, until they have an opportunity to compare it with the Ruins of Athens, drawn upon the spot by an English artist, who will soon oblige the world with a publication.

69. *LM*, XXIX, August 1759, pp. 432–434 (excerpt from *The Ruins of Athens*, Sayer ed.: "Account of the ACROPOLIS or castle of ATHENS").

70. *BSW*, 1759, V, Part 1, pp. 181–185 (review):

. . . Der Titel allein kündiget schon die Schönheit des Unternehmens an, and so vortheilhaft auch die Vorstellung ist, die man sich davon macht, so übertrifft es doch noch weit unsre Erwartung.

Der historische Theil der Kunst läszt nichts zu wünschen übrig, weder von Seiten des Beobachters, noch von Seiten des Zeichners. Die einselnen Theile sind von einer bewundernswürdigen Feinheit, und die Schönheit des Stichs des Zeichnungen würdig. Herr LE ROI hat auf ewig die verstümmelten, doch kostbaren Reste dieses Griechenlands, das heut zu Tage halb eine Wüste, und halb eine Barbarey ist, den Verwüstungen der Zeit entrissen.

. . . Da endlich diese Monumente der Griechen verschiedenen sehr dunkeln Stellen im VITRUV ein sehr groszes Licht geben, die durch den PERRAULT verstümmelt worden, so hat Herr LE ROI sie zu erklären, und richtig zu erläutern gesucht. . . .

71. *NAE*, April 1760, pp. 193–211 (review):

. . . Ita hic noster, quem merito et impense laudes, Franco-gallus, *le Roy*, ipsam artium omnium parentem terram ingressus, superstites illic spendidissimorum aedificiorum ruinas doctis et curiosis oculis listravit, earumque contemplandarum copiam omnibus iam facit, qui Opere pulcherrimo, sed eodem tamen cariore, frui potuerint. . . .

Laudandi vero Auctoris non hunc demum locum capiemus, cum videamureum satis ipsa recensionis continuitate laudasse. Scribendi genere puro utitur, neque ineleganti, inprimisque ad amoenitatem argumentis conciliandam idoneo. Requirant forsitan iure nonulli Latinum potius sermonem in huius inenii opere, quan Francogallicum. Nam illa perspicuae et concinnae narrationis lumina, quibus quasi illustrari aeterna Graecae Romanaeque antiquitatis monumenta debent, unde nisi a Latinis litteris expectanda sunt? Sed tamen cum Architecto artis suae inter paucos peritissimo, Graecorumque et Romanorum librorum minime ignaro, non agemus severius. Considimus certe, hos eius Commentarios non leviter commendaturos cum lectoribus omnibus, tum popularibus inprimis ipsius, doctae antiquitatis studium, quod horum hodie pars admodum tenuis, Francogallos volumus, accurate et spienter tractare nobis quidem videtur. Est autem opus omne non solum charta et litterarum formis, sed lineis etiam ab Auctore ductis, dein beneficio laminarum aenearum expressis, adeo nitidum et comtum, vix et illi pulchrior quaedam species tribui potuerit.

72. James Adam to Helen Adam, 16 November 1760 (see below, entry 95).

73. A. F. P. Marigny to C. Natoire, 21 September 1762 (Jean Monval, *Soufflot . . .*, Paris, 1918, p. 502):

Les dessins du sieur Le Roy et du sieur Chalgrin sont assez bien; mais je voudrais que nos architectes s'occupassent plus qu'ils ne le font des choses relatives à nos moeurs et à nos usages que des temples de la Grèce: ils s'éloignent de leur objet en se livrant à ce genre d'architecture; je ne juge point cette étude aussi favorable pour cultiver et augmenter leurs talents qu'ils peuvent le penser.

74. J. J. Winckelmann to J. J. Barthélemy, 13 September 1760 (Winckelmann, *Briefe*, Berlin, 1952–1957, II, p. 101):

En parcourant les Monumens de M. Le Roy j'aurois souhaité qu'il ait vu les temples de Piesti ou Pesto, et pour la troisieme Epoque de l'ordre Dorique le Prostile tout entier d'un temple Dorique à Cori, Ville située vers Veletri. . . .

75. *BSW*, IX, 1763, pp. 1–8 (excerpt from part two of LeRoy's *Ruines*.)

76. *JS*, August 1768, pp. 3–10 (review of LeRoy, *Observations* . . . , Paris, 1767):

M. le Roi regarda cet Ouvrage [*AA*] comme une copie du sein, parce que tous les desseins & toutes les descriptions étoient conformes à ce qu'il avoit rapporté, & qu'il n'en différoit que par des fautes & des altérations.

. . . M. le Roi n'avoit pas dessein de donner tous les monumens d'Athénes, mais seulement les plus beaux, comme son titre l'annonce, & ce reproche conviendroit mieux aux sçavans Anglois, dont le but étoit plus général & qui cependant ont négligé pendant leur voyage de rassembler tout ce qu'il y avoit.

Ces mêmes sçavans reprochent encore à M. le Roi de n'avoir pas développé comme eux différéntes parties des monumens & quelques profils. M. le Roi avoit déjà répondu à ces omissions prétendues, en annonçant qu'il ne détailleroit pas également les édifices ou leurs parties & qu'il se bornoit à ceux qui étoient assez beaux pour être imités ou qui pouvoient servir à l'Histoire de l'Art.

Quelques petites différences qui se rencontrent entre les mesures sont encore un objet de critique, mais le but de M. le Roi étoit de connoître le rapport des monumens des Grecs entre-eux avec ceux des Peuples qui les ont précédés ou suivis, & avec ceux que décrit Vitruve: il les a mesurés, dit il, avec la plus grande exactitude sous ce point de vue, & non pour observer les rapports de ces édifices & de leurs parties avec les divisions de notre pied. D'ailleurs un même profil mesuré par les hommes très-exacts avec des pieds d'inégale longeur produit toujours des différences.

Si M. le Roi a donné moins de planches de détails que les Voyageurs Anglois, c'est qu'il s'est fait un mérite de les réduire à la plus petite quantité possible & qu'il a cru qu'il étoit inutile de donner une planche de chacune des figures qui ornent les frises & de plusieurs mauvais profils; il s'est borné aux plus beaux, en un mot, il a fait un choix.

Quand on examine les différences qui sont entre l'Ouvrage Anglois & celui de M. le Roi, on voit que l'un ne peut jamais tenir lieu de l'autre; M. le Roi observe que les vues ont été mal prises par les Anglois, qu'elles n'offrent que des amas confus au milieu desquels les monumens sont en quelque façon cachés; qu'au contraire il s'est attaché à faire dominer l'édifice principal, afin qu'on pût le distinguer mieux des accessoires, & pour cela il a choisi le lieu le plus commode pour son point de vue.

77. C. L. Clérisseau, *Monuments de Nîmes*, Paris, 1778, pp. xiij–xiv:

. . . il étoit réservé de vérifier les Antiquités de la Grece, à un Amateur distingué, qui dans la fleur de la jeunesse & jouissant de tous les avantages que peuvent donner une illustre naissance & de grands biens, s'est arraché aux délices de Paris, pour entreprendre un voyage long & pénible: après avoir surmonté les obstacles de ce voyage, il en procure l'agrément au Public, en mettant sous ses yeux le tableau pittoresque de la Grece. Qu'il me soit donc permis de le remercier au nom des Arts, & de le proposer pour exemple à ceux qui peuvent en les cultivent leur rendre comme lui les services importans.

78. C. N. Cochin, *Mémoires inédits* . . . , Paris, 1880, "M. le Comte de Caylus (1692–1765)", pp. 78–79:

. . . M. LeRoy, architecte pensionnaire du roy eut occasion de faire un voyage en Grèce, il y croqua les antiquités qu'il y trouva; mais ses desseins étoient si informes que, quand nous les vîmes à Paris, nous eûmes peine à croire qu'on en pût tirer quelque chose. M. de Caylus, chaud amateur de la Grèce ainsi que de l'Egipte, les fit redessiner par Le Lorrain qui, quoique peintre très-médiocre et manqué malgré les plus belles dispositions, néanmoins dessinoit agréablement et avec goust. Il vint à bout d'en tirer les desseins que l'on a gravés; on peut juger de là du degré de fidélité et combien on peut se rapporter aux détails de cet ouvrage.

Il étoit question de faire graver les planches; c'étoit une dépense au-dessus des forces de M. Le Roy, à moins qu'on ne les fit à très grand marché; cependant on vouloit qu'elles fussent bien gravées. On ne pouvoit pas mieux choisir que le fit M. de Caylus en s'adressant à M. LeBas; mais il fallut encore qu'il usast de toutte son éloquence persuasive pour engager Le Bas à les graver pour la moitié moins qu'elles ne valoient, en lui faisant cependant entrevoir quelque dédommagement si le livre réussissoit. Le livre s'est bien vendu, mais la gratification n'est pas venue. Aussi M. Le Bas, qui sait très bien compter et qui n'est pas mal attaché à ses intérests s'en est-il toujours plaint.

1760   **RUINS . . . AT SPALATRO**, Proposal

79. *BSBA*, III, Part 1, January–March 1760, p. 209 (summary and notice):

. . . Soixante Planches *in Folio* gravées par les plus grands maîtres, composeront cet ouvrage, où l'on trouvera des vues perspectives de la ville de Spalatro, du Palais & des lieux circonvoisins, comme aussi les plans, élevations, sections, & bas-reliefs de ce superbe édifice. Le tout accompagné d'une Introduction qui renferme une description du Plan général de ce Palais, & de la façon dont les Anciens arrangoient leurs appartemens, avec plusieurs observations sur la manière qui règne dans leur architecture. L'Auteur de ce bel ouvrage est ROBERT ADAM, Architecte,

... Ceux qui ont acquis les *Ruines* de *Palmyre* & de *Balbec*, qui répondirent si bien à ce que le Public attendoit de leur très-ingéieux Editeur, seront encouragés à souscrire actuellement une Guinée & demie pour celles que nous annonçons, & à payer la même somme en recevant l'ouvrage. ...

80. *JE*, 15 March 1760, pp. 153–154 (notice).

81. *BSW*, VII, Part 1, 1761, p. 142 (notice).

82. *JS*, March 1762, pp. 238–239 (notice).

1762   **ANTIQUITIES OF ATHENS**

83. J. D. LeRoy to A. C. P. Caylus, 7 April 1755 (François Sèvin, *Lettres sur Constantinople* ..., Paris, an x [1802], pp. 102–109):
... Les étrangers qui voyagent ici ont obligation à MM Stuard et Rivet. Ils ont découvert à Athènes des trésors cachés sous la terre ou dans d'épaisses murailles, et je ne doute point que leur ouvrage ne soit fort exact et fort beau.

84. J. J. Barthélemy to A. C. P. Caylus, 10 December 1755 (see entry 29 above).

85. J. J. Barthélemy to A. C. P. Caylus, 20 December 1755 (Barthélemy, *Voyage en Italie*, Paris, 1801, p. 61):
J'ai vu les premières épreuves des Ruines d'Athènes par les Anglais. Elles m'ont paru très-bien exécutées, et m'ont confirmé dans mon sentiment dont je vous ai fait part.

86. T. Gray to W. Mason, 8 June 1756 (Gray, *Correspondence* ..., ed. Toynbee and Whibley, Oxford, 1935, II, p. 463):
... I rejoice to hear the Prints succeed so well, & am impatient for the work, but do not approve the *fine Lady* part of it. What business have such people with Athens? ...

87. Robert Adam to Janet Adam, 30 March 1757 (ERO, GD18/4833):
If John woud sett off directly & meet me at Vicenza we woud go at his expences in a Vessell from Venice directly to the Greek Islands which is a pleasant Saill of 8 days & from that we'd go to Athens. In short taking Clerisseau & my two Draughtsmen with us two, we would furnish a very tolerable Work to Rival Stuart & Rivets in 3 months time & return home laden with Laurel. ...

88. Robert Adam to James Adam, 1 November 1757 (see entry 28 above).

89. T. Gray to T. Wharton, 21 February 1758 (Gray, *Correspondence*, Oxford, 1935, II, p. 565):
... I am told that ... Stuart's Attica will be out this spring ...

90. Robert Adam to James Adam, 11 August 1758 (ERO, GD18/4850):
... Rooker I hope will do the front of the temple of Jupiter which you was pre-

sent at the formation of. It turns out a Showy Drawing; & that & the Inside of said Temple if well engraved ought not to be ashamed of Palmyra or Balbec whatever it may be of the Tower of the Winds or Lanthorn of Demosthenes. . . . That insignificant trifling ingorant puppyish Wretch Basire, has spoilt me a plate entirely. it is the outside of the little sqr Temple, which is hard, ill drawn, of a Bad Colour, in short I have a mind to throw it in his Hands, as unworthy of appearing in my Work. You remember those he did for Stuart, This was rather Worse I suppose Stuart has bribed him, he's quite a sicofantish creture of his, & I think this will be rather severe, deeming him unfitt for my work, who has done so much of Stuarts.

91. *CR*, VIII, July 1759, pp. 70–82 (see entry 68 above).

92. W. Chambers, *Treatise on Civil Architecture*, London, 1759, p. 36:
   . . . the Antiquities of Athens, lately published by Mr. Le Roy, (and of which we may soon hope to see another very perfect account, illustrated with a great number of beautiful Plates, by Messrs. Steward and Ryvet) . . .

93. Robert Adam to James Adam, 24 July 1760 (ERO, GD18/4866):
   Stuart you see will never Publish More, Le Roy has done no justice, why thin might no we have taken up the cudgils & why would he out of a peice of idle Vanity prostitute these Antiquitys to people, who are fixt friends to Mr Blackfriars & who never chuse to look me in the face. Nor show not the smallest enclination to see me or subscribe, or any thing else. . . . Mr Hall was here one day lately & told us Mr Wood & Mr Ramsay & all of them had only obtained 30 Subscribers to Mr Irwins Baths so that they have Delayed it till next Winter to try what it will produce and if they continue to be so unsuccessful I suppose they will give it up. This is Somewhat astonishing & makes me wonder the less at my Subscriptions not answering my expectations though Princes in Comparison. Before any new publication I should wish for a Truce & Cessation, as every body complains of the Frequency of these Works. A Peace will also turn mens minds more to the Arts, & works of Merit. I am persuaded that if Stuart had to begin his Subscriptions as he has happily for himself ended them he would not procure 100 in London.

94. James Adam to Betty Adam, 17 September 1760 (ERO, GD18/4872):
   . . . If Mr S——t corrects his own plates I am not surpris'd that he is slow in giving his designs, for he undertakes most tedious Labour.

95. James Adam to Helen Adam, 16 November 1760 (ERO, GD18/4876):
   . . . I do not understand Glenirot nor his notions in the smallest degree, even here they begin to think they are never to see the English Athens. As to the French one probability is that it is extremely incorrect, as we found LeRoys measures of the Temple of Pola very inexact. And the fellow who was not there but one day, has the impudence to say that there was no other thing but this Temple of Pola, that

merited being given to the Publick. Bob can judge if the Amphitheatre & Trium-
phall Arch are so undeserving of publick attention.

96. James Adam to Janet Adam, 14 March 1761 (ERO, GD18/4890):
. . . The Athenians, Sicilians & Chineze are asleep You say, & make no noise in
the world, let them rest . . .

97. J. J. Winckelmann to J. J. Volkmann, 27 March 1761 (Winckelmann, *Briefe*,
Berlin, 1952–1957, II, p. 131):
Von den Alterthümern von Griechenland des Herrn Stuart is der erste Band
heraus, aber noch nicht in Rom erschienen. Strange, welcher einige erhabene
Arbeiten darzu gestochen, ist itzo hier, und man schätzet ihn für den besten
Kupferstecher, der in der Welt ist.

98. William Hogarth, November 1761 (engraving):
The Five orders *of* PERRIWIGS, *as they were worn at the late* CORONATION, *measured*
Architectonically. Advertis[e]ment. *In about* Seventeen Years *will be compleated, in*
Six Volumns, folio, price Fifteen Guineas, *the exact measurements of the* PERRIWIGS *of the*
ancients; *taken from the Statues, Bustos, & Baso-Relievos of* Athens, Palmira, Balbec,
and Rome *by* MODESTO Perriwigmeter *from* Logôdo. *None will be Sold but to*
Subscribers. Published as the Act directs Octr 15, 1761.

99. James Adam to Janet Adam, 12 June 1762 (ERO, GD18/4936):
. . . Strange arriv'd here a few days ago from Naples. I had a long visit of him
yesterday & among other pieces of intelligence, I learnt that he had been inform'd
by Sr. J———s, thro' the Coll I suppose, that at last Glen Iriot was prepair'd for the
Publick, & that we shou'd see him presently dedicated to H. M. whose leave for
that purpose was obtain'd. I don't know if this piece of news has yet arous'd Gros.r
Street, but I can't say I lik'd this sort of forstalling much I wish we had been first,
you may remember I wrote you of my fears on this head some time ago. However
I am far from saying this interferes with our project, because why not two of these
to the protector of arts? & perhaps there may be something cleverer in the one,
than in the other which I shou'd be extremely desirous of.

100. Robert Adam to James Adam, 12 January 1762 (see entry 112 below).

101. P. J. Mariette to G. G. Bottari, 7 August 1762 (Bottari, *Raccolta di lettere* . . .
Milan, 1822–1825, IV, pp. 371–372):
. . . Io non c'impiegherò per certo il mio danaro, e amo meglio spenderlo,
come ho fatto, nel primo tome delle *Rovine d'Atene* pubblicato adesso in Londra
dal sig. *Stuart*. Io non posso lodarvelo abbastanza, e non credo, che in questo
genere si sia fatto cosa di più bello. Tutto è giudizioso, e ben ragionato, e nulla
fondato su le conghietture. Ecco come io vorrei, che tutti quelli, che vogliono
ravvivare le antiche memorie, facessero, e non spacciassero per verità i capricci, che
sono passati loro per la testa dormigliando.

102. J. J. Winckelmann, *Anmerkungen über die Baukunst der Alten*, Leipzig, 1762, pp. B2 *v*–B3 *r*:

Die mehresten Tempel und Gebäude in Griechenland hat Herr le *Roy* im Jahre 1759. theils bekannt gemacht, theils genauer gezeichnet und beschrieben. Im Jahre 1750. im Monate May unternahmen zween Maler aus England, Hr. *Jac. Stuart*, und *Nic. Revett*, nachdem sie einige Jahre in Rom ihre Kunst getrieben, die Reise nach Griechenland. Ihre Freunde in England brachten einen hinlänglichen Beytrag zusammen, Zu Beförderung dieses Vorhabens, und dieses was ein Vorschusz oder eine Pränumeration auf die Beschreibung, welche sie machen würden, Einige zahlten auf viele Exemplare dieses Werkes voraus, und der Anschlag war etwa auf zwo Guineas, des Stück, gemachet. Gedachte kunstler brachten des erste Jahr ihrer Reise mehretheils zu *Pola* und in *Dalmatien* zu, wo sie alle Ueberbleibsel des Alterthums genau abzeichneten. Das folgende Jahre giengen sie nach Griechenland, u. verbleiben deselbst fast an vier Jahre: sie kamen im Monate Decemb. 1754. nach Marseille zurück. . . . *Dawkins* war nach seiner Rückkunft in England ein groszmüthiger Beförderer der Beschreibung der Alterthümer von Griechenland, und Herr *Stuart* genosz in dessen Hause zu London alle Bequemlichkeit, seine Zeichnungen in Kupfer stechen zu lassen, wozu er sich zween geschickter Künstler, Herrn *Strange* und Herrn *Bezaire* bedienet. *Dawkins* starb vor ein paar Jahren in der Blüte seines Alters, und seine Tod ist ein Verlust für die Künst und Wissenschaften. Die Arbeit an dem Werke von Griechenland wurde fortgesetzet; es erschien der Plan von demselben, und es waren schon vor swen Jahren die Kupfer zu dem ersten Bande geendiget. Dieses Werk erwartet man itzo mit groszem Verlangen: Denn es wird weitläustiger und ausfuhrlicher werden, als die Arbeit des Herrn le *Roy* ist, weil jene so viel Jahre, als dieser Monate, in Griechenland gewesen sind.

103. T. Gray to W. Mason, 6 March 1763 (Gray, *Correspondence*, Oxford, 1935, II, pp. 798–799):

You may remember, that I subscribed long since to Stuart's book of Attica; so long since, that I have either lost or mislaid his receipt (wch I find is the case of many more people) now he doubtless has a list of names, & knows this to be true. if therefore he be an honest Man, he will take two guineas of you, & let me have my copy (and you will chuse a good impression) if not, so much the worse for him. by way of *douceur* you may, if you please (provided the subscription is still open at its first price) take another for Pembroke-Hall, & send them down together: but not unless he will let me have mine; & so the worshipful Society authorise me to say. . . .

104. *MR*, XXVIII, April 1763, pp. 302–308 (review):

It is many years since the ingenious Authors of this elegant and accurate work formed the design of visiting Greece, in order to take exact admeasurements and delineations of such remains of ancient Architecture, as might be found still subsisting in the city of Athens and the country adjacent; a design for which every lover of the fine arts then admired their spirit and resolution, as much as we must now applaud the care and attention evidently bestowed in the execution of it.

. . . Mr. Le Roy's work, it is true, is greatly superior in point of scenery; his views are beautifully picturesque; the drawings executed with taste, and the engravings masterly. In this respect, the present work [*AA*, I] is most defective; the general views are stiff, and indifferently designed. . . .

In the capital and most essential parts of this undertaking, however, our English Artists indisputably bear away the palm. In the preservation of the due proportions in the architectural parts of the works, Le Roy can hardly be named in comparison; his shameful negligence in taking his measures, or carelessness in laying them down, being evident on sight, to those who have any knowledge of architecture.

On the whole, we esteem this volume as a very valuable acquisition to the Lovers of antiquities and the fine arts; and, hoping soon to see a completion of the work, we recommend it as a proper companion to those noble descriptions of Palmyra and Balbec, by Mr. Dawkins and Mr. Wood; those Gentlemen having early encouraged our Artists in the prosecution of a design so worthy of the most distinguished patronage.

105. *JE*, 15 April 1763, III, Part 2, pp. 142–144:

. . . Il n'en est pas de même des morceaux rapportés dans cet excellent ouvrage; tout en est curieux, exact dans les détails, utile aux Artistes, agréable pour les Littérateurs, & très-intéressant pour tous ceux qui sont nés avec quelque goût pour les Arts. . . .

106. *AReg*, VI, 1763, pp. 247–249:

. . . The work of messieurs Stuart and Revett is, in every respect, as original and informing, as if no other on the subject had gone before it. Indeed, that which has preceded it [LeRoy's *Ruines*] rather afforded new and powerful reasons for the publication of this. The numerous and important mistakes, with which that book is filled, both in the disquisitions and designs, had rendered more exact enquiries, and more accurate drawings, absolutely necessary.

The work before us carries the most evident marks of truth and exactness. The labour employed in it must have been immense. We do not remember ever to have seen any work, which manifests so much ingenuity in the researches, and which discovers, at the same time, so guarded and punctilious an accuracy with regard to facts, on every thing which related to measurement and design. . . . In perusing this work, the reader will observe with pleasure that there is not a single monument treated of, which is not set in a light absolutely new.

107. *JE*, 1 September 1764, VI, Part 2, pp. 118–121 (*"Observations sur les Athèniens modernes, tirées des Antiquités d'Athènes*: par J. Stuart, A Londres, 1764.").

108. J. J. Winckelmann to H. Fussli, 22 September 1764 (Winckelmann, *Briefe*, Berlin, 1952–1957, III, p. 57):

Es ist der erste Band der *Antiquities of Greece* von Mr Stuart hier angekommen; findet aber eben so wenig als in Engeland Beyfall. Denn dieser ganze grosze erste Bande fangt an mit Kleinigkeiten wie der Thurm der Winde ist, wo alle Figuren auf groszen Blättern gestochen sind, und man siehet, es hat ein groszes Buch werden sollen. *Monstrum horrendum ingens, cui lumen ademtum.*

109. *BSW*, XI, Part 1, 1764, pp. 117–123 (review):

. . . Endlich können wir den Liebhabern der Alterthümer und besonders der Baukunst die Ausgabe eines wichtigen Werks ankündigen, das man als die Folge der prächtigen Ruinen von Palmyra und Balbec ansehen kann, ob es gleich ganz andre Vefasser hat. Es wurde bereits vor mehr als 15 Jahren dazu Hoffnung gemacht. Die Freunde von denen Ruinen redeten so vortheilhaft davon, dasz man mit Ungedult darauf wartete, um zu sehen, ob Frankreich oder England sich eines bessern Werks in Dieser Art wurde zu rühmen haben.

. . . Zu Anfange und Ende eines jeden Kapitels sind statt der Vignetten, Münzen, oder neue Monumente und Inscriptionen, die den Tert erläutern, gedruckt. Die architectonischen Ausmessungen sind sehr genau und grosz vorgestellt: sie machen aber das Werk auch sehr kostbar.

1764   **RUINS . . . AT SPALATRO**

110. James Adam to Margaret Adam, 24 September 1760 (ERO, GD18/4873):

. . . I had a letter from Johnie by last post . . . He seems to think that tis very material to have Bob's book finish'd soon, so as not to disappoint the Subscribers by a delay, which he says there have of late been so many instances of, that he finds the people even in Scott. are shy on that account, & wou'd therefor be glad to show them that no delay was intended on this occasion. If however Bob promises himself considerable advantage by putting off for a twelve month, I think he may safely take that Liberty without offending the publick much, & I own I shou'd think the delay not only an advantage to him but to the Book.

111. James Adam to William Adam, 30 September 1760 (ERO, GD18/4784):

. . . Now perhaps You will think the state of these Subscribers is somewhat particular, for You must know there is no such thing as drawing money from them before they see the Book, & even then perhaps they shrink at the near approach of what they view'd with indifference at a distance, so that I don't believe one half of them will purchase the Book, but I thought it was not at all amiss to have their names at any rate, as they are many of them high sounding & will read well in England. . . . These [titles of potential Italian subscribers] might be translated, but as people are fond of things misterious it may perhaps be as well to keep them in the Original Tongue.

112. Robert Adam to James Adam, 12 January 1762 (ERO, GD18/4922):

. . . as yet I know nothing more hear nothing of any of my plates which distress

I

me infinitely as People begin to cry out on me as they did on Stuart, so that I am afraid of becoming his appology . . .

113. James Adam to Janet Adam, 16 January 1762 (ERO, GD18/4923):
. . . The other half sheet, he will see, is the last words of Spalatro, who cou'd have conceiv'd it wou'd have drag'd on to this time.

114. James Adam to Janet Adam, 12 June 1762 (see entry 99 above).

115. J. J. Winckelmann to J. J. Volkmann, 18 June 1762 (Winckelmann, *Briefe*, Berlin, 1952–1957. II, 237–238):
Es wird in kurzen ein prächtiges Werk in Englischer Sprache, vermutlich in Italien, gedruckt werden, welches genaue Zeichnungen des Pallasts des Kaisers Diocletianus zu Salona in Dalmatien, nebst den Tempeln und andern Ueberbleibseln zu Pola und an andern Orten in Illyrien enthält. Der Verfasser ist Adam, ein junger und sehr reicher Engländer, welcher Baumeister, Zeichner und Kupferstecher auf seine Kosten hält. Die Kupfer zu diesem Werke sind in seiner Wohnung in Rom gestochen. Der Bericht darzu in Englischer Sprache, welchen er mir durchzusehen gegeben, ist mit vielem Verstande und Geschmacke entworfen. Es stehet derselbe im Begriff, auf seine Kosten eine Reise nach Griechenland, durch die ganze Levante und durch Aegypten zu thun. Ich könnte sein Gefährte seyn, wenn ich wollte.

116. J. J. Winckelmann to Francke, 26 June 1762 (Winckelmann, *Briefe*, Berlin, 1952–1957, II, p. 243: summary of entry 115).

117. J. J. Winckelmann to L. Usteri, 4 July 1762 (Winckelmann, *Briefe*, Berlin, 1952–1957, II, p. 248).
Es sind hier zwey Engländer welche in Begriff stehen, grosze Reisen zu unternehmen: einer heiszt *Adams*, ein gemeiner *Squire*, welcher einen erfahrnen Baumeister, einen geschickten Kupferstecher und ein paar Zeichner auf seine Kosten unterhält und mit ihnen nach Griechenland gehet. Es gibt deselbe in viel prächtigen Blättern den Pallast des Diocletianus zu Salona heraus, und deszen Bericht dazu im Englischen, welchen er mir im MS. mitgeheilet hat, ist geschrieben wie ich hätte zu schreiben gesuchet. . . .

118. Betty Adam to James Adam, 21 December 1762 (ERO, GD18/4950):
. . . Bob is perfectly sick of all publications especially by subscription, as he has full experienc'd by his own work that people look upon it as picking their pockets which to be sure is not an agreeable way for a gentleman to make money these things are at present a Drug & he does not think that they are likely to have soon a greater relish for them the french designs he is of opinion woud not be better receiv'd than any other work the only thing he says is something quite new that has never been seen nor that they have any hope to see.

119. James Adam to Helen Adam, 15 January 1763 (ERO, GD18/4956):

[Betty] speaks of Bobs being sick of Publication by Subscription, which I'm sure I shall be the last person to propose another attempt of the same kind, what I mean by future Publications is merely in the volunteering way, make the work interesting & let them purchase who will.

120. *BSBA*, XXII, Part 1, July–September 1764, pp. 202–203 (review):

. . . Cet ouvrage . . . est d'autant plus intéressant, qu'il ne nous reste presque d'autres monumens de l'Architecture Grecque & Romaine, que des Bâtimens Publics, tels que des Temples, des Bains, & des Amphithéatres, qui par leur solidité ont résisté aux injures du temps.

121. *JE*, 15 August 1764, p. 130 (notice).

122. *CR*, XVIII, October 1764, pp. 296–299 (review):

We congratulate the public on the noble and numerous list of subscribers prefixed to this work, and we are sorry to observe, that the engraved part of it is done by foreigners, with a taste and execution that never has been equalled in this country. . . .

Having thus done justice to this magnificent work, and, we hope, to the abilities of its editor, our readers will not suspect us of any malevolence, when we say, that the architecture of it is not comparable to that of Dioclesian's baths. . . . strong as our veneration is for the works of antiquity, we cannot help thinking . . . many . . . English noble personages, are more elegantly as well as more comfortably lodged than the emperor Dioclesian was when he inhabited this superb edifice. Upon the whole, we cannot adopt the high idea which Mr Adam endeavours to give us of this emperor's taste; for the disparity between this place and his baths seems to render it accidental, and that it pointed rather towards state and magnificence than true gracefulness and beauty.

123. *GL*, IV, 30 December 1764 (Suppl.), pp. 65–74 (review):

Les Amateurs de l'Architecture doivent de la reconnoissance à l'Auteur de ce magnifique Ouvrage aussi intéressant par l'objet même qu'il met sous nos yeux que précieux par la beauté de l'exécution. . . .

Les bâtimens des anciens, dit ce savant Architecte, sont pour l'Architecture ce que les Ouvrages de la nature sont pour les autres Arts. Il nous présentent à la fois le modele & la regle. Aussi tous ceux qui prétendent acquérir un certain degré de supériorité, soit dans la théorie soit dans la pratique de l'Architecture, ont-ils senti la nécessité de voir par eux-mêmes ce qui nous reste des anciens édifices, pour y puiser ces idées de grandeur & de beauté que peut-être ces Ouvrages seuls peuvent inspirer. . . .

124. P. J. Mariette to P. M. Paciaudi, 8 February 1765 (Caylus, *Correspondance*, Paris, 1877, II, p. 324):

. . . Avez-vous vu le beau livre qu'on vient de publier à Londres et qui contient en une soixantaine de planches les antiquités de Spalatro . . . C'est un ouvrage qui ne le cède point pour la beauté de l'exécution aux antiquités de Palmyre et de Balbec . . .

125. *JS*, April 1765, pp. 396–399 (review):

Après avoir déjà donné au public les Ruines de Palmyre & de Balbec & les Antiquités d'Athènes, l'Angleterre, par les soins de M. Adam, contribue encore aux progrès des Arts & des Lettres, en publiant les Ruines du Palais de Dioclétien à Spalatro. Les Edifices publics des Anciens Grecs & Romains, comme leurs Temples, leurs Thermes, leurs Amphithéâtres, se faisoient remarquer sur-tout par leur solidité. Mais combien d'édifices particuliers, par leur commodité & par leur elegance? Le temps a respecté en partie quelques-uns des édifices du premier genre; à peine a-t-il laissé quelques traces des autres, auxquels nous ne pouvons néan-moins refuser notre admiration sur la foi des Historiens. On ne connoîtra cependant jamais bien toutes les beautés de l'Architecture Ancienne, modele de la nôtre, tant qu'on ignorera les richesses qu'elle a sçu étaler dans la construction des édifices particuliers. On ne peut donc qu'applaudir au dessin de M. Adam, & lui sçavoir gréer de l'exécution.

126. P. J. Mariette to G. G. Bottari, 12 October 1765 (Bottari, *Raccolta di lettere* . . . , Milan, 1822–1825, V, pp. 282–283):

. . . Non è necessario, che voi abbiate un corrispondente in Londra, per farvi venire le Antichità di Spalatro. Il *sig. Clarisò*, che le ha disegnate, dimora in Roma, e ve le procurerà. Non trascurate di farne acquisto. Il libro è degno della vostra curiosità. . . .

127. G. G. Bottari to P. J. Mariette, 16 October 1765 (Bottari, *Raccolta di lettere* . . . , Milan, 1822–1825, V, p. 286):

. . . No ho per anco vedute le *Antichità di Spalatro*, ma le procurerò, perchè saranno belle. . . .

128. *BSW*, XII, Part 1, 1765, pp. 90–98 (review):

. . . Für Baukünstler würden keine Denkmäler in der Welt von gröszerm Werthe und Brauchbarkeit seyn, als solche Privatgebäude, indem keine Beschreibung eines Schriftstellers hinreichend ist, die Vertheilung, Gestalt und innre Einrichtung, Bestimmung und Gebrauch aller und jeder Piecen, vollkommen verständlich zumachen. . . .

. . . Es ist kein Zweifel, dasz nicht Baukunstverständige zu vielen neuen Ge-danken Stoff und Veranlassung darinnen finden sollten. In der Angebung und Bestimmung der Nahmen so wohl als des Gebrauches der einzelnen Zimmer dürfte man vielleicht etwas Willkührliches anzutreffen glauben. Allein, bey üherer Vergleichung mit dem Vitruv findet man, dasz Herr Adams letzterm ganau gefolget ist.

1768 **THE GRECIAN ORDERS OF ARCHITECTURE**

129. *BSBA*, XXVIII, Part 2, October–December 1767, pp. 501–502 (notice):
. . . L'Auteur, qui a voyagé dans l'Asie & dans la Grèce, établit dans cet Ouvrage, d'après les Ruines de la Grèce, les mesures & les caractères des Ordres Dorique, Ionique, & Corinthien, & les met en parallèle avec ceux de *Palladio*, de *Scamozzi*, & de *Vignole*, qui sont ceux des Modernes qui ont profilé avec le plus de netteté. . . . ce qui doit sur-tout donner un idée avantageuse de l'Ouvrage, c'est qu'il a l'approbation de Mr. *Stuart*, qui a si exactement mesuré & décrit des Antiquités d'Athènes.

130. *CR*, XXV, May 1768, pp. 345–354; September 1768, pp. 161–169 (synopsis).

131. *NBSW*, VII, 1768, p. 176 (announcement).

1769 **ANTIQUITIES OF IONIA**

132. W. Chambers to Lord Charlemont, 4 February 1770 (*Manuscripts and Correspondence of Charlemont*, London, 1891–1894, I, p. 298):
. . . The dilettanti book is published, and a cursed book it is, between friends, being composed of some of the worst architecture I ever saw; there is a degree of madness in sending people abroad to fetch home such stuff. I am told this curious performance has cost the society near three thousand pounds; such a sum well applied would be of great use and advance the arts considerably, but to expend so much in order to introduce a bad taste is abominable. However, not a word of all this to any dilettante living.

133. *CR*, XXIX, February 1770, pp. 119–127 (notice):
[The Society of Dilettanti gives] preference to the revival of Greek architecture in its purest stile. . . .

134. *BSBA*, XXXIV, Part 2, October–December 1770, pp. 461–464 (notice):
. . . l'on a commencé par les Antiquités de l'Ionie, parce, qu'après l'Attique, c'est peut-être le Paye qui merite le plus l'attention des Antiquaires.

135. *NBSW*, X, Part 2, 1770, pp. 358–359 (review).

136. *MF*, September 1771, pp. 182–183 (review):
L'accueil que le Public a fait à quelques ouvrages dans ce genre, a engagé plusieurs amateurs en Angleterre, de se cotiser pour faire lever, dessiner ou recueillir tout ce qui peut encore subsister de monumens dans l'ancienne Gréce, capables de jetter du jour sur l'histoire de ce pays célèbres . . . on a joint aux vues qui représentent l'état actuel de ces temples, tous les détails des chapitaux, des bases de colonnes, des entablemens, des bas reliefs & des ornemens que l'on peut encore distinguer; ce qui rend cet ouvrage à la fois curieux & instructif.

137. *NBSW*, XII, Part 2, 1771, pp. 222–240 (review).

138. H. Walpole to Mary Berry, 25 September 1791 (*Horace Walpole's Corres-pondence*, New Haven, 1944, XI, Part 1, pp. 357–358):

... They who are industrious and correct, and wish to forget nothing, should go to Greece, where there is nothing left to be seen, but that ugly pigeon-house, the Temple of the Winds, that fly-cage, Demosthenes's lanthorn, and one or two frage-ments of a portico—or a piece of a column crushed into a mud wall—and with such a morsel and many quotations, a true classic antiquary can compose a whole folio and call it Ionian Antiquities! ...

139. Correspondence of N. Revett with the Society of Dilettanti (Society of Dilettanti Letterbook 1736–1800, pp. 274–277):
(a) The case of Nicholas Revett humbly submitted to the Consideration of the Society of Dilettanti [by Revett].

The Society having come to a Resolution to consider of publishing the remain-ing Materials collected by Dr. Chandler Mr. Pars and myself in our Voyage to Asia Minor and Greece, permit me in this Manner to lay before the Society the State of my Case in regard to them, and humbly to submit it to their Candour and Human-ity.

As many Members of the Society have been elected since, and may not be thoroughly acquainted with the Transactions which passed relative to the publica-tion of the Produce of our Expedition to Asia Minor and Greece; I beg leave to observe that the Society having at their Expence paid for setting the Letter-press and engraving the Plates of the Ionian Antiquities, came to a Resolution not to proceed upon that Plan in regard to the remaining Materials, but to put them into our hands for publication, hoping the Sale of the Ionian Antiquities might be such as to enable us to convey them likewise to the Public.

Upon this the Journal with Inscriptions was given to Dr. Chandler to publish as belonging to his department; the Bas Reliefs of the Temple of Minerva at Athens to Mr. Pars; as were the following subjects, selected out of the Architectures, to me, for the same purpose (viz) The Propylea and the Arch of Hadrian at Athens; the Temple of Minerva at Sunium; the Temple of Jupiter Nemens in Achaia; the Temple of Ceres and Proserpine at Eleusis; the Gymnasium at Ephesus; the Temple at Jackli near Mylasa; the great Theatre at Laoidcea, and the Column of Menander at Mylasa.

When I set out on this Expedition I was flattered with hopes the Society would procure for me some small provision at my return, which with the desire of making myself a useful Servant of the Society, were the Motives for my engaging in this Undertaking: nor were my hopes ill grounded as is evident from the Society having favoured me with a Letter to Lord North upon the publication of the Ionian Antiquities, recommending me to his Notice and Protection, and setting forth that a valuable Collection of Drawings in Architecture would be lost to the Public, if I was not supported. Which Letter I had the Honour to present to his Lordship accompanied with a Copy of the Ionian Antiquities as a specimen of my labours.

Had this produced the desired Effect, I should have been enabled to have accomplished the Work committed to my charge; as I then could have made it my sole Object, and have devoted my money to the execution of it, and being sensible of the good Wishes of the Society towards me should have engaged in the Task with pleasure and Satisfaction. But failing of success from his Lordship, and in the Sale of the Ionian Antiquities, by which I have greatly suffered hitherto, not having disposed of half the Impression though I have used my utmost Efforts both at home and abroad, I find the publishing the above Work in Numbers, which plan I had the Honour to mention to Sir William Hamilton will be attended with such great and heavy Expence together with so little prospect of advantage, that I dare not venture to undertake it, unless the Society will, by procuring for me some Office or Salary, enable me to carry it into execution, which I humbly submit to their Consideration.

(b) To the Society of Dilettanti [by Revett]:

Having been informed by Lord Le Despencer of the uneasiness that was expressed at the last Meeting of this Society on the first Sunday of last month, at my not having finished and delivered in to the Society all the Drawings of Architecture, the Materials of which were collected by me during the last Journey I made into Greece, in company with Doctor Chandler and Mr. Pars.

The State of the Case is this, Doctor Chandler published his book of Inscriptions, and our Journal by Subscription (as I am informed) and he reaped the Benefit. Mr. Pars drew the Views which are now in the hands of the Society; and the Basso Relievos in the Frize round the Cell of the Parthenon were left with him to publish for his own Benefit. These Relievos (I am informed) have been since lost, by his attempting to carry them abroad, a loss to this society and the Curious. He has farther received the generous appointment to sixty pounds a year, for three years, from the Society. The Profits from the sale of the Ionian Antiquities were given equally to Doctor Chandler, Mr. Pars, and myself. The Society paid for engraving the Plates, and setting the Letter-press; and we three paid for paper and printing six hundred Copies, which cost us upwards of fifty nine pounds each. The Society printed for themselves one hundred and fifty, which they disposed of as they judged proper. A hundred and fifty out of the six hundred Copies, which we printed, were sold at one Guinea and half each: or to explain it farther, we took each of us ten Copies, and sold one hundred and twenty, out of which must be deducted the Expences of numerous advertisements, and for the Book-sellers profits: so that those hundred and twenty did not pay our Expences of Paper, printing and disposing of them. The remaining four hundred and fifty I unfortunately and imprudently purchased and gave Doctor Chandler, and Mr. Pars one hundred pounds each. Since that time I have not disposed of one hundred and fifty, and have been obliged to hire a Room to preserve all my remaining copies; so that altho' it is nine years and upwards since I purchased these copies I remain still out of Pocket.

From the time we left England to our return was very near two years and a half, and I was allowed for Clothes, pocket money, and all my labour, risk, and fatigue, two hundred pounds. And soon after we returned in November 1766, the Society was pleased to give us four hundred pounds, which for my share came to one hundred thirty three pounds six shillings and eight pence, and from that time to the year 1770, when the Book came out, I was employed in making the Drawings of the Ionian Antiquities, in over looking the Engravers, Copper-plate Printers, and in other Services attending that Work, for which I had no further Considerations from the Society altho' I paid twenty pounds out of my own pocket for an unfinished Engraving, a View of the temple of Jupiter Panellenius, which belongs to the Work I am now about, which Plate was began before the Society had determined not to go on with publishing the Work themselves.

I beg leave to refer to a Letter dated March the 4th, 1774[?], which I wrote to Mr. Crowle the then Secretary, and is now in the Possession of the Society, wherein I mention my having finished near one half of the Drawings—which amount in number to forty seven. I now have finished thirty five, and am going on with the remainder; in the mean time I must try to get some Employment in order to subsist, having consumed my little paternal fortune in travelling. By the powerfull Interest of this Society, I do flatter myself, that some annuity may be procured for me, or granted to me (being in the Decline of Life) to enable me to finish this Work, which I still hope the Society will have engraved and published at their own Expence. However awkward it is for a man to speak of himself, I hope I may venture to say, I have planned and directed the Execution of some few Buildings, which I trust will not disgrace me as an Architect. . . .

Projects and publications of Paestum and Sicily

1750s   **PAESTUM** Project (Conte Gazola)

140. J. J. Barthélemy to A. C. P. Caylus, 20 December 1755 (Barthélemy, *Voyage en Italie*, Paris, 1801, pp. 55–60):

J'ai remis à M. le comte de Gazolles la lettre de M. Leroi. Je Vous en remercie en mon particulier: mais nous avons été également surpris d'une anecdote qu'elle contenoit; c'est que M. Cochin ou M. Soufflot va donner le plan du temple de Poestum. Il faut que vous soyez instruit de la part que M. le comte de Gazolles prend à cette nouvelle, et que vous jugiez vous-même.

Il est le premier qui ait eu une connoissance exacte de ces ruines. Son premier soin fut de se porter sur les lieux; il y mena des architectes qui en levèrent le plan sous sa conduite. Déterminé à les faire graver, il y est retourné plusieurs fois, et compte au printemps s'y rendre de nouveau, pour prendre quelques détails qui lui manquent encore. Il a non seulement le plan de ces temples, mais le developpement de toutes les parties dessinées avec bien de l'exactitude et de la sagacité. Le tout doit être vérifié de nouveau ce printemps, après quoi il les fera graver tout de suite, et les accompagnera d'une explication qui contiendra tout à la fois des remarques sur l'architecture et des éclaircissemens de littérature: voilà le projet de M. le comte de Gazolles. Tout Naples, tous les étrangers en étoient instruits, et tout le monde savoit qu'il étoit fort capable d'exécuter cette entreprise.

Cependant M. Soufflot vient à Naples; il apprend de M. de Gazolles qu'il y a des ruines d'architecture à Poestum; il voit les plans que ce dernier en a fait lever. Il temoigne quelqu'envie de voir ces monumens; M. de Gazolles lui facilite le voyage, et lui donne ses architectes pour l'accompagner. M. Cochin lui promet, de son côté, de graver ou de faire graver à Paris, sous ses yeux le plan du temple. M. de Gazolles le lui confie, et c'est après toutes ces peines, tous ces voyages, toutes ces dépenses, qu'on lui écrit de Paris, plusieurs années aprèsqn'on va graver le plan due temple, et qu'on se flatte de s'être rencontré avec les architectes de M. de Gazolles. Que pensez-vous de ce procédé? Je vous prie, mon cher comte, de n'en faire aucun bruit: mais vous pouvez rendre service à un galant homme, et j'ose vous dire que vous le devez. Tachez d'empecher qu'on ne fasse paroître à Paris le plan de Poestum, tel qu'on l'a dans cette ville; c'est l'intêret de ceux qui l'on entre leurs mains. Quand ils auront donné ce plan, en seront-ils bien avancés? Il n'ont pas les développements et les détails. Du reste, je dois vous observer que M. de Gazolles ne leur sait pas mauvais gré de leur projet; il est persuadé qu'il y a du mal-entendu dans cette affaire, et qu'on cru apparemment qu'il avoit abandonné le dessein de publier les antiquités de cette ville. Vous n'en serez pas quitte pour cette premier démarche.

141. LeRoy, *Ruines*, Paris, 1758, p. x, note b:

. . . M. le Comte de Gazole, Commandant de l'Artillerie du Roi des deux Siciles, doit bientôt les donner tous au Public. M. Soufflot . . . en a fait voir ici plusieurs Plans très-curieux qu'il a dessinés sur le lieu avec beaucoup de soin.

142. *BSW*, V, Part 1, 1759, pp. 168–169:

. . . Ein andres wichtiges Werk für die Liebhaber der Alterthümer und der Baukunst wird gleichfalls dieses Jahr erscheinen. Der Graf von GASOLES läszt nämlich die treflichen Ruinen zu PESTO accurat abzeichnen und stechen, und mit seiner gelehrten Erklärung drucken. . . . Das merkwürdigste sind 3 Tempel, wovon noch ganze COLONNADEN stehen: man bewundert darinnen nicht so wohl die Architecktur der höchsten Zeit, als vielmehr eine schöne Proportion, und edle Einfalt.

143. A. C. P. Caylus to P. M. Paciaudi, 12 October 1761 (Caylus, *Correspondance*, Paris, 1877, I, p. 263):

. . . [Soufflot] m'avait aussi donné quelques vues de Pestum qu'il avait faites avec le comte de Gazzola. A propos ce galant homme, que devient cet ouvrage dont il était si occupé? Je n'entends plus parler.

1764   **SUITTE DE PLANS . . . DANS LA BOURGADE DE POESTO . . .** (Dumont)

144. A. C. P. Caylus to P. M. Paciaudi, 26 December 1764 (Caylus, *Correspondance*, Paris, 1877, II, p. 66):

   . . . Quoique ces planches ne soient pas bien exécutées, je vous en voie celles qu'on a gravées de la ville de Paestum. M. le comte de Gazzole s'en était occupé autrefois et avait voulu les donner au public. Soufflot les avoit dessinées le premier. Je ne sais qui a dérangé tout cela. Enfin elles ont paru et peuvent vous amuser . . .

145. *PV*, 17 December 1764, p. 191:

   . . . il y a des détails intéressans & des morceaux d'Architecture qui en font connoitre la véritable origine. . . .

146. G. G. Bottari to P. J. Mariette, 5 November 1765 (Bottari, *Raccolta di lettere . . .* , Milan, 1822–1825, V, p. 288):

   . . . Se qualche dilettante d'antichità volesse provvedersi di quelle di *Pesto*, se ne trovano varj esemplari in Roma per vendersi a uno scudo Romano.

147. *Mémoires de Trévoux*, October 1766, pp. 187–189 (review: similar to entry 145 above).

148. *AL*, 10 July 1766, V, pp. 263–264 (review):

   . . . Mrs *Soufflot & Franque* . . . ont vû avec plaisir que M. *Dumont* a mis au jour des Plans & élévations des Temples de *Paestum* ou *Possidonia*, qui sont d'autant plus importans pour l'Architecture, qu'ils donnent connoissance de l'Ordre Dorique dans des temps plus rapprochés de son origine.

1765   **SEI VEDUTE DELLE ROVINE DI PESTO** (Morghen)

1767   **THE RUINS OF POESTUM** (Berkenhout)

149. *JE*, 15 November 1767, VIII, Part 1, pp. 79–85:

   Cet ouvrage fait honneur aux talens & au goût de l'Anonime, qui, en le publiant, à rendu un important service aux Antiquares & aux Artistes.

150. *LM*, XXXVI, December 1767, p. 636 (review).

151. *AReg*, X, 1767, pp. 137–139 (review):

   . . . How astonishing soever it may seem, that such very considerable remains of ancient magnificence should have continued totally undiscovered during so many centuries, it is nevertheless most certain that the author of this book is the first traveller who has given us any account of the ruins of Poestum.

1768   **THE RUINS OF PAESTUM . . .** (Major)

152. *BSBA*, XXX, Part 2, October–December 1768, pp. 469–474 (review):

   . . . il peut aller de pair avec ceux qu'on a publiés sur les Ruines de Palmyre & Balbec. . . . Les vues des deux premières Planches ont été dessinées sur les lieux, en préférence de Mr. *Jacques Gray*, Envoyé d'Angleterre. Les dessins des Temples ont été faits à Naples par ordre d'un Anglois, qui n'est point nommé, mais à qui on doit en grande partie toute l'entreprise de ce bel Ouvrage. Les plans, les élévations & les mesures sont les mêmes qui se trouvent dans l'Oeuvre de Mr. *Dumont*, & sont dus, comme nous l'avons dit plus haut, à Mr. *Soufflot*, de la générosité & de la politesse duquel le Graveur de Londres se loue beaucoup. . . .

153. *NBSW*, VII, Part 1, 1768, pp. 177–178 (review):

. . . Diesz von uns schon bey Gelegenheit der drey andern über die Ruinen von Poestum im leszten Stücke de Bibliothek angekündigte Werk ist nunmehr erschienen. Der plan ist viel weitläustiger, als bey jenem englischen Werke, und die Ausführung ist so, dasz des Verfassers Ruhm, den er sich bereits als ein braver Künstler erworben, nicht um ein geringes vermehret.

154. *NBSW*, VII, Part 1, 1768, pp. 285–293 (review).

155. *MF*, January 1769, pp. 171–172 (review):

Ce volume, imprimé avec beaucoup de soin & de dépense, contient une dissertation sur l'origine de Paestum, ainsi que sur son état ancien & moderne; la description des temples de cette ville avec plusieurs remarques utiles, & des explications sur les monnoies & médailles de Paestum conservées dans différens cabinets d'Angleterre & représentées dans l'ouvrage. On est redevable à M. Soufflot, de l'académie royale d'architecture de Paris, des plans, élévations & dimensions des édifices de Posidonie. Cet habile architecte les avoit levés sur les lieux avec la plus grande exactitude, & il a bien voulu les communiquer à M. Major pour l'exécution de son entreprise. Le nom de ce graveur Anglois, qui s'est formé en France & s'est déjà fait connoître par plusieurs bons ouvrages sortis de son burin, doit inspirer toute confiance sur le mérite des graveures que nous annonçons.

Ce magnifique ouvrage convient non-seulement aux sçavans, par les recherches historiques & critiques dont il est rempli, mais encore aux artistes & aux amateurs de la belle architecture, à ceux [s]ur-tout qui ayant déjà les ruines de Palmyre & de Balbec par MM. Wood & Dawkins; les monumens de la Gréce, par M. le Roi; les antiquités d'Athènes, par MM. Stuart & Revett, veulent connoître les premiers progrès de l'architecture chez les Grecs, nos maîtres dans les beaux arts. Les temples de Paestum sont les monumens les plus précieux de leur ancienne architecture & les mieux conservés.

1769   **LES RUINES DE PAESTUM** . . . (Dumont: Berkenhout text).

156. *MF*, June 1769, pp. 191–193 (review):

. . . M. Dumont . . . est entré dans de plus grands détails. Il a donné des plans exacts, ainsi que des élévations géométrales . . . gravés d'après les dessins de M. Soufflot, & suivant les mesures que ce célébre artiste en prit en 1750. Ce dernier ouvrage peut donc être regardé comme un supplément à celui de M. Thomas Major. M. Dumont est le premier qui ait fait connoître par la graveur, les fameux temples de Paestum, les monumens les plus anciens & les mieux conservés de l'architecture grecque dans son aurore.

157. *JS*, October 1769, pp. 336–344 (review):

Cet ouvrage n'interessa pas moins les Amateurs de l'Architecture ancienne, que les Sçavans; les premiers y trouveront des réflexions sur l'origine & les progrès de l'Architecture & principalement sur l'Ordre Dorique, les seconds des recherches sur une ancienne Ville & plusieurs Inscriptions.

158. *NBSW*, X, Part 2, 1770, pp. 182–184 (review).

ANTIQUITIES OF SICILY Project (Mylne)

159. R. Mylne to Mr Mylne, 28 January 1758:

. . . By your delaying always since we came to Rome first, you have gained 8 months on us in allowing £30 a year cash, which our nessityes could never have allowed you to have done, had it not been for my expedition into Sicily with Mr. Phelps, by which I both saved & gained enough of Money to set us free of the world. Therfore from this I infer, that you will immediately this last favour, as I expect to go home this ensuing autumn, but in the mean time will pursue this affair with Mr. Phelps to see if any thing will through up to put me into the world, if not I can always have recourse to the first intention. . . .

160. R. Mylne to William Mylne, 26 April 1758:

. . . my atachment to Mr Phelps was not with an intent to pass more time in Italy with him entirely for pleasure, but that I might have these drawings to do of the antiquities of Sicily after I came to London, which would very apropos fill up a gap in my time before I fell into business, and perhaps even help my doing so: Altho at the same time I have too sincere a gratitude for Mr. Phelp's goodness to me, not to make him the towell alone to raise my fortune, without making any return. I only differ in opinion about his morals or heart, because you don't know him. I presume you have heard the Character of the Welch in general to be, immoveable in their hatred and friendships. . . . This then was the reason that he carried his enmity so far against Mr Nulty, and his friendship for me.

161. R. Mylne to William Mylne, 16 December 1758:

. . . My old friend Mr. Phelps . . . has spoken nothing to me as yet of finishing his Antiquities of Sicily for publishing, but I expect to get them to do when I return to London, as it will fill up some vacant time very well.

162. R. Mylne to William Mylne, 18 January 1759:

. . . [Mr Phelps] is gone lately to Naples, and at parting we agreed that I should begin the Antiquities of Sicily for publishing immediately on my return to London.

163. R. Mylne to William Mylne, 11 February 1759:

. . . I am at present searching out for a draftsman to be sent into Sicily very soon to do over again what was done by Nulty, he [Phelps] has sent me likewise a letter to Nulty clearing me of any underhand play towards him. . . .

164. James Adam to Helen Adam, 11 November 1760 (ERO, GD18/4876):

... Sir Thos. told me that Milns told him he had gon to Sicilly to take the Ruins there, & that he was to publish them presently, & can he afford all this Is he like you a Man of fortune. or is this the insolence of the fellow. I told him the truth that I never had heard of his fortune, & that he had gon to Sicilly at the expence of Mr. Philps alongst with one Nolty a fan painter, & that I supposed it was Mr. Phelps that would publish what he had pay'd for.

APPENDIX III

EXCERPTS FROM THE NOTES OF
SIR WILLIAM CHAMBERS

How distant the Grecians were from Perfection in Proportions in the Art of Profiling & I may venture to say in the whole Detail of the Decorative Part of Architeckture will appear at first Sight to every one whether Ignorant or informed who unprejudiced compares the Columns, Capitals, Bases Pedestals, Entablatures & Ornaments in the Works of Messrs le Roy, Revet & Stewart and other ingenious travelers with the Antiquities of Rome which those who have not had or are not likely to have an Opportunity of seeing in the Originals may find in Palladio, Serlio, Desgodets, Sandrart, Piranesi & many other Books in which they are delineated with sufficient accuracy But should any Man be diffident of his own Judgement, or trusting to the Encomiums of a few Ingenious but too partial Travellers, discredit the Testimony of his own Eyes, he cannot have a more corroborating Proof of the Imperfection of the Grecian Architecture than that it is diametrically opposite in almost every Particular to that of the Romans, whose Works have been admired, copied & imitated by all the great Architects from the fourteenth Century when the antient Stile of Architecture began to revive, till this Day, although these great Architects were by no means unacquainted with the Grecian Manner of Building Calabrea, Sicily & even Rome furnished Examples, which had they deserved the Preference would no doubt have been copied or had they deserved Notice would at least have been mentioned in their Work besides Greece & its Antiquities are not a discovery of Yesterday. Accounts of them were published in the last Century & when Desgodets was employed to measure the Antiquities of Rome other Artists were sent for the same purpose to Greece, had what they collected there merited a Publication it would probably have made its Appearance in the World a hundred Years ago.

But supposing for Argument Sake that the Grecian Architecture was intrinsically more perfect than the Roman yet the Fashion or habit of Admiring the latter is of so long a standing our Prepossessions are so strong in its favor & its Reputation is established upon such indisputable Authority that it would be almost impossible to remove them, a general Outcry of Artists & Connoisseurs would perhaps bring even the Gothic Architecture into Vogue again, & might cheat us into a Reverence for Attic Deformity but the Opinions of two or three or half a dozen can have but little Weight in a matter of this Nature, they might with equal success oppose a Hottentot & a Baboon to the Apolllo & the Gladiator as set up the Grecian Architecture against the Roman the *Ton* in anything is not easily given and it would be as absurd to suppose that Monsieur or Mr. such a one should turn the torrent of

Prejudice in any particular Branch of Art as it would be to imagine that a Peasant could set the Fashion of a dress. Things that do not admit of absolute Demonstration are measured by the number and Reputation of those that adopt them & either esteemed or despised in Proportions as they are well or ill protected.

It hath afforded Occasion of Laughter to every intelligent Architect to see with what Pomp the Grecian Antiquities have lately been ushered into the World & what Encomiums have been lavished upon things that in Reality deserve little or no Notice, it is however to be lamented that these Encomiums ill grounded as they are, have made strong Impressions on many ingenious Men chiefly Men of Learning who accustomed to admire and to taste the Beauties of Grecian Literature have easily been persuaded into a belief of Grecian Superiority in an Art of which they were themselves no Judges, A few Remarks upon some of these celebrated Trifles may here be permitted they are not made with any invidious Design but merely to set them in a proper light, & with an Intent to undeceive such as have been led astray by fine words & elegant Publications.

The celebrated Lantern of Demosthenes or Choragic Monument of Lysicrates or the Temple of Hercules with all its other Names is in Reality not quite so large as one of the Centry Boxes in Portman Square its Form and Proportions resemble those of a silver Tankard excepting that the Handle is wanting. Messrs. Steward & Ryvet have given twenty six Plates of this Edifice well drawn & well engraved in which all its Parts are represented with the utmost Accuracy & from an Inscription upon the Architrave it appears that this Monument was erected in the Days of Alexander the Great when the Grecian Arts were at the highest Pitch of Excellence so that we may look upon this Building as a Cryterion of the Grecian Taste in Architecture when its utmost Perfection which as the learned Architect will perceive bore a very exact Resemblance to the Taste of Boromini universally & Justly esteemed the most licentious & Extravagant of all the modern Italians.

The celebrated Temple of the Winds or Tower of Andronicus Cyrrhestes to vulgar Eyes resembles exactly one of the Dove houses usually erected on Gentlemens Estates in the Country of England, excepting that the Roof is somewhat flatter & there is no Turret for the Pigeons to creep in & fly out at, but we are assured that a more nice observer will be greatly pleased with its Elegance & extraordinary Beauty the Republic of Arts has been enriched with nineteen Plates of this wonderful Monument for which the Publi [word illegible] ained the Designs with exceeding [word illegible] Labor & Expence the Account of the Opperation begins like that of a regular Siege & is as follows, "the first was a trench along the South East Side where at the Depth of about fourteen feet the upper Step appeared and after that two others and at length the Pavement the trench was then carried round the Angle at the Southern Extremity of this Side with an Intention to continue it likewise along that Side which fronts the South but there the Workmen were soon stopped by a Wall which projected from it & which appeared evidently to be an Original Part of the Building on further Search it was found to be built on a Plan which is about three fourths of a Circle & to project from the South Side of the Octagon after the manner of a modern Bow Window, the next Place that seemed to demand some Attention was on the North West Side where there remained some faint traces of the Door &c" they tell us that by removing two thousand seven Hundred Cubical feet of Stones & dirt they discovered the Inside Pavement which was all of White Marble & that by pulling down a House & afterwards building it up again they had an Oppotrunity of drawing the whole figure of Libis & half of Notus including his Books.

Indeed None of the trifles now existing in Greece although so pompously described and Elegantly represented in Several late publications seem to deserve much notice—either for Size or taste of Design nor are they in any Way calculated to throw new lights upon the Art or to contribute in the least towards its advancement, not even those said to be erected by Alexander the famous Parthenon or Temple of Minerva built in the Acropolis of Athens, during the Government of Pericles when the Grecian Arts flourished most was no very surprizing Work although it excited the Murmurs of all Greece & had for its Architects Phidias, Callicartes & Ictinus. the Onions & Radishes distributed to the Workmen during the Building of one of the Pyramids amount to twice the Sum expended upon this whole temple many of our Parish Churches are much more considerable Buildings & by a very exact Calculation I find St. Pauls of London just three & forty times as large exclusive of a fraction of 247,384598; With Regard to the Stile of its Architecture it is too imperfect to deserve a serious Criticism.

We find indeed in antient Writers very pompous Descriptions of the Ephesian Temple of Diana & of several Other Temples of Greece but they are in general stuff & with so many absurdities that little faith ought to be given to them and if the Grecian Architecture was imperfect in the Days of Pericles & Alexander surely it must have been much more so four or five Hundred Years before about which time this Ephesian Temple may be supposed to have been built. the Panegyrics of Poets & Historians in Works of Art are not always to be relyd upon read Pope & Jervais was another Apelles look at his Works and you find him a mere sign Painter even so it was in antient Times writers were often biassed by Friendship or Prejudice & sometimes misled by Ignorance.

At first Sight it appears extraordinary that a People so renowned for Poetry, Rhetoric, & every sort of Polite Literature and who carried Sculpture farther than any of the antient nations should be so deficient in Architecture yet upon Reflection many Reasons will suggest themselves to us why it naturally should be so.

Greece a Country small in itself was divided into a Great Number of little States none of them extremely powerful populous nor Rich so that they could attempt no very considerable Works in Architecture neither having the Space nor the Hands nor the Treasures necessary for that Purpose it must be owned Says Monsieur d'Ablancourt that Grece eaven in the Zenith of its greatness had more ambition than Power we find Athens flattering herself with the Conquest of the Universe though unable to Deffend her own territories against the Incursions of her neighbors and we find despairing reduced to sue for peace upon the loss of four hundred men. the Lake of Moeris would have drowned Peloponessus and beggard Greece, Babylon only one of the many famous cities, with which the Assyrian Empire abounded would have covered Attica, & more Men were employed to build it than there were inhabitants in all the Grecian States the Egyptian Labyrinth was an hundred times larger than that built in Imitation of it by Dedalus in Crete & there is more stone in the great Pyramid than there was in all the Public Buildings of Athens, if we recollect at the same time that whilst divided into many Governments Greece was constantly harressed with domestic Wars and from the time of its union under Phillip always in an unsettled State that an uncommon Simplicity of Manner prevailed amongst the Grecian Nations & that the Strickest Maxims of Equality were jealously adhered to in most of their States it will be easy to account for the little Progress the Grecians made in Architecture Demosthenes observes that the Houses of Aristides, Miltiades or any other of the great Men at that Time were no finer than those of their Neighbors such was their Moderation & so steadily did they adhere to the antient Manners of their Country one of the Laws of Lycurgus ordained that the Ceilings of Houses should only be wrought by an Ax.

What little Magnificence the Grecians then displayed in their Structures was confined to public Buildings which were chiefly Temples in which there appears to have been nothing very surprizing either for Dimensions or ingenuity of contrivance. Greece almost constantly the Theatre of War abounded not like Italy in magnificent Villas where the richest Productions of the Pencil & Chizel were displayed, their Roads were not adorned with Mausoleums to commemorate their Heroes, nor their Towns with Arches to celebrate their Triumphs, the Grecian Theatres were trifling compared with those of Italy the Numachia and Amphitheatres unknown amongst them as were also the Thermini in which the Romans displayed so much splendor.

In later times indeed the Greeks & chiefly the Athenians abated their original Severity the Orator above mentioned observes that in his Time there were some private Houses more magnificent than public Edifices but this does not appear to have been very common & therefore could occasion no great additional Splendor even Alcibiades the most luxurious Greek of His Time, the Macaroni of the Day for he wore a purple Cloak and slept on a Bed with a canvass bottom doth not seem to have been better lodged than the rest of the Athenians excepting that his house was painted. but as it was the work of one man done most probably in a short time (since the Artist was clandestinely kept prisoner all the while) we may fairly conclude that either the house must have been very small or the Performance very imperfect.

It will perhaps be alledged that as the Greeks brought the Arts of Painting & Sculpture to Perfection they must necessarily have done so with Architecture likewise it being closely connected with them, but that is by no means a consequence for both Sculpture & Painting are much more easily cultivated than Architecture & being in a great Degree Arts of Imitation & having in a great measure their Cryterion in Nature they would of course make quicker strides towards Perfection than Architecture which has no such guides.

Architecture is a creative Art & that of a very complicated kind the hints which it collects from Nature are rude & imperfect a tree is the model of a Column a basket & a Dock Leaf those of a Capital & a hut is the Original of a Temple, the precise form, the exact Proportion, & degree of Strength, with a thousand other Particulars are left to the Determination of the Art & can only be attained by a number of Experiments & a long Series of Observations not easily made but in times of profound Peace in Countries where Wealth abounds & where Splendor prevails.

Since therefore it appears that the Grecian Structures are neither the most considerable not the most varied in the World & since it has been proved as clearly as the Nature of the Subject will admit that they are not the most perfect it naturally follows that our knowledge ought not to be collected from thence but from some purer & more abundant Source and this in whatever relates to the Ornamental branch of the Art can be no other than the Roman Antiquities still existing in Italy, France & many other Countries remains of Buildings erected in the politest Ages & by the Richest most Splendid & most Powerful People in the World who after having transported to Rome from Carthage, Sicily & Greece the rarest Productions of the Art of Design as also the ablest Artists of the Times were constantly employed during many Centuries in the Construction of all kinds of Buildings that either Use, Convenience or Pomp requires, & must therefore have improved upon the Grecian Architecture & carried the Art to a very high degree if not to the highest degree of perfection. . . .

. . . Nature is the Supreme & Ultimate Model of the imitative Arts upon which every great Artist must finish his Idea of the Profession in which he means to excell The Antique is to the Architect what Nature is to the painter or Sculptor the Source from whence his chief Knowledge must be collected and the model upon which his Taste must be formed.

But as in Nature few Objects are faultless so neither must it be imagined that every antient Production in Architecture eaven amongst the Romans was perfect or a fit Model for Imitation as some Blind Adorers of Antiquity would insinuate, on the Contrary their Remains are so extremely unequal that it will require the greatest Circumspection and Effort of Judgement to make a proper Choice, the Roman Arts like those of other Nations had their Rise their Era of Perfection and their decline at Rome as in London or Paris there were few great Architects & many very indifferent ones and they had their Connoisseurs as we have ours who sometimes would dictate to the Artists and cramp the happy Sallies of their Genius, or Force upon the world their own insipid Productions, promote ignorant Sycophants and discourage and even oppress honest Merit. . . .

In the Constructive Part of Architecture the Antients were no great Proficients. I believe many of the Deformities which we observe in the Grecian Buildings must be ascribed to their Ignorance in this Particular such as their Gouty Columns their narrow Intervals their disproportionate Architraves their Ipetral Temples which they knew not how to cover and their Temples with a Range of Columns running in the Center to support the Roof contrary to every Rule both of Beauty and Conveniency.

THE PLATES

1. Temple (from Wood, *Balbec*)

2. Elevation (from Wood, *Palmyra*)

3. Ceiling (from Wood, *Palmyra*)

4. R. Adam. Ceiling, Osterley Park

5. Pola. Temple (from Stuart, *Antiquities*)

6. London. Cavendish Square

7. Athens. Tower of the Winds (from Stuart, *Antiquities*)

8. Athens. Tower of the Winds (from LeRoy, *Ruines*)

9. Athens. Monument of Lysicrates (from Stuart, *Antiquities*)

10. Athens. Monument of Lysicrates (from LeRoy, *Ruines*)

11. Shugborough. Tower of the Winds

12. Shugborough. Monument of Lysicrates

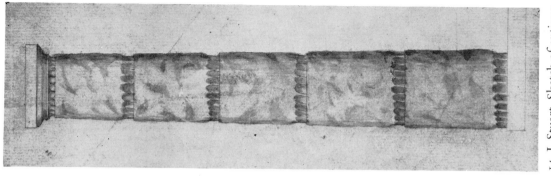

14. J. Stuart. Sketch of antique column

13. Shugborough. Shepherd's Monument

15. Plessis–Chamant. Pump house

17. J. Stuart and W. Newton. Pulpit, Greenwich Hospital

16. J. Nollekens. Monument to William Weddell

18. J. Wyatt. Radcliffe Observatory

20. J. Soane. Holy Trinity, Marylebone

19. J. Elmes. St John's Chapel, Chichester

22. D. R. Roper and A. B. Clayton. St Mark's, Lambeth

21. W. and H. W. Inwood. All Saints', Camden Town

24. C. F. Porden. St Matthew's, Lambeth

23. W. and H. W. Inwood. St Pancras, London

26. Mr Clarke. St Margaret's, Brighton

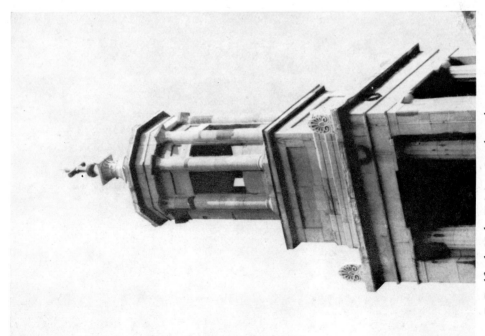

25. F. Bedford. Holy Trinity, Southwark

27. Corinthian Order (from Wood, *Balbec*)

28. Ionic Order (from Stuart, *Antiquities*)

29. Corinthian Order (from Stuart, *Antiquities*)

30. R. Adam. Portico, Royal Society of Arts

31. Ionic Order (from LeRoy, *Ruines*)

32. R. Adam. Ionic Order, Great Hall, Syon

33. Corinthian Order (from Stuart, *Antiquities*)

34. D. Burton. Charing Cross Hospital

35. C. N. Ledoux. Portico, Salines

36. Le Camus de Mezières. Pagoda, Chanteloup

37. Portico (from LeRoy, *Ruines*)

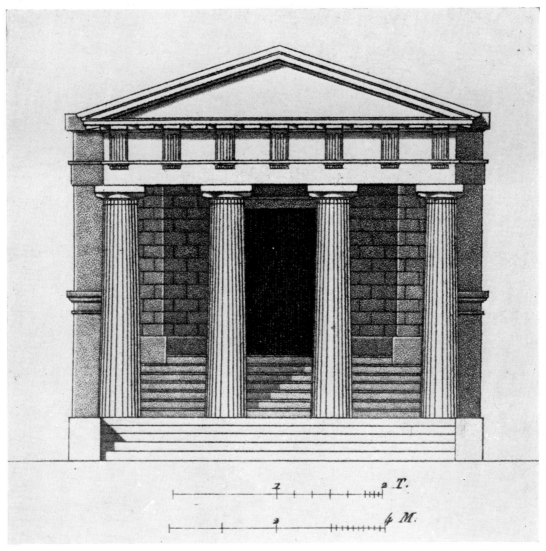

38. J. Antoine. Portico, Hôpital de la Charité

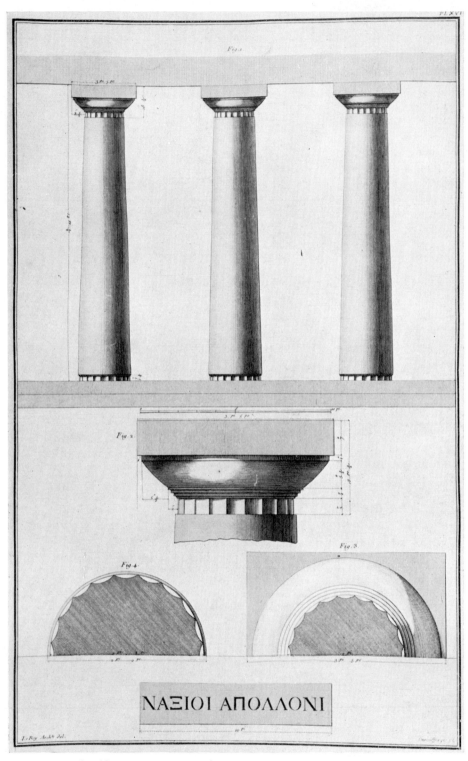

39. Doric Order (from LeRoy, *Ruines*)

Fig. 3.

Fig. 1.

Fig. 4.

Fig. 2.

40. Doric and Tuscan Orders (from LeRoy, *Ruines*)

41. F. J. Bélanger. Courtyard, 11 rue de la Victoire

42. A. T. Brongniart. Cloister, Couvent des Capuchins

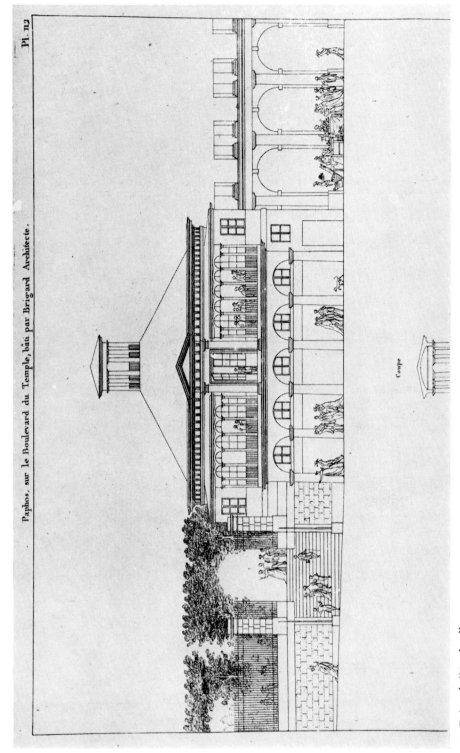

Pl. 112

Paphos, sur le Boulevard du Temple, bâti par Brigard Architecte.

Coupe

43. Bricard. "Paphos"

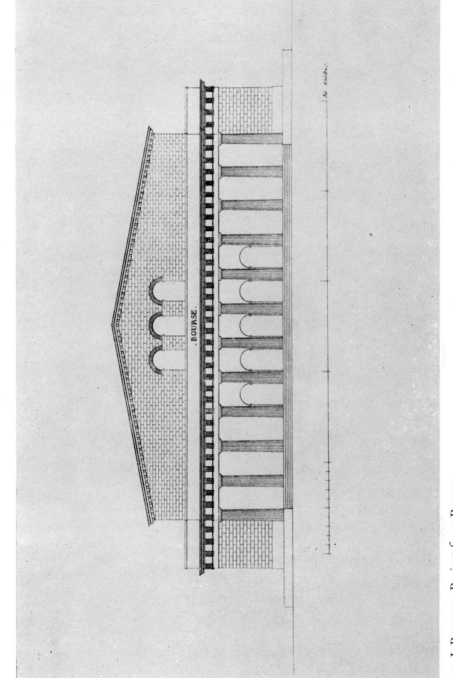

BOURSE.

44. J. Pompon. Project for a Bourse

45. N. Revett. East Porch, Trafalgar House

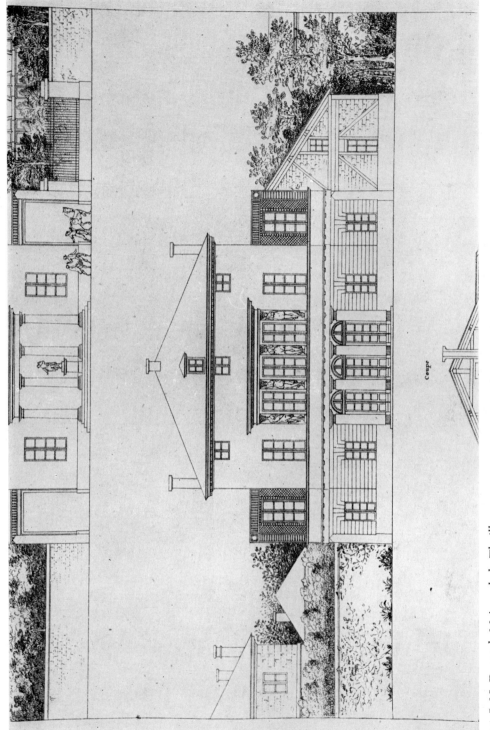

46. J. N. Durand. Maison de la Thuille

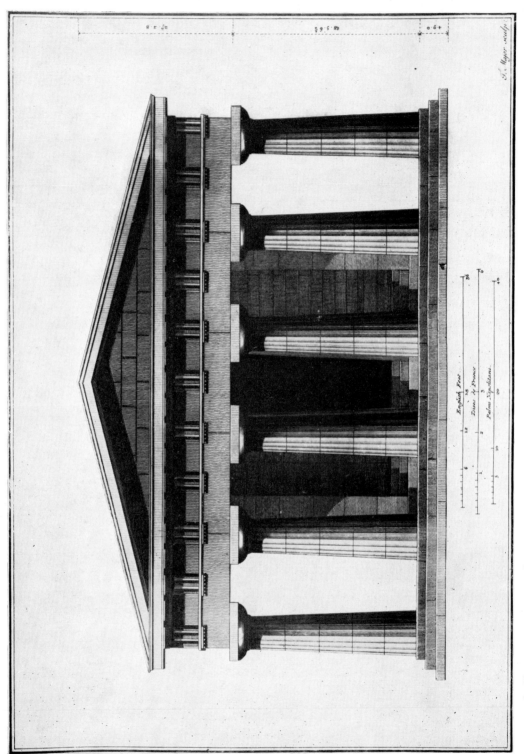

47. Temple (from Major, *Paestum*)

48. J. Soane. Project for a Canine Dog House

49. T. Johnson. Warwick County Gaol

50. J. Soane. Barn à la Paestum

51. G. Dance II. Portico, Stratton Park

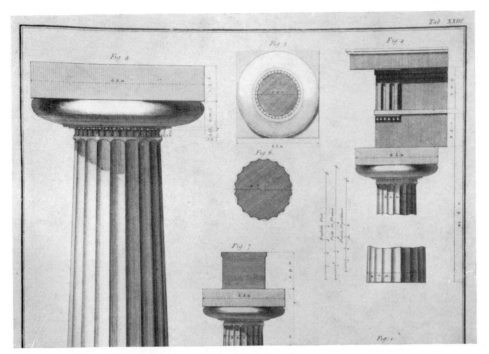

52. Doric Order (from Major, *Paestum*)

53. B. Latrobe. Doric Order, Hammerwood House

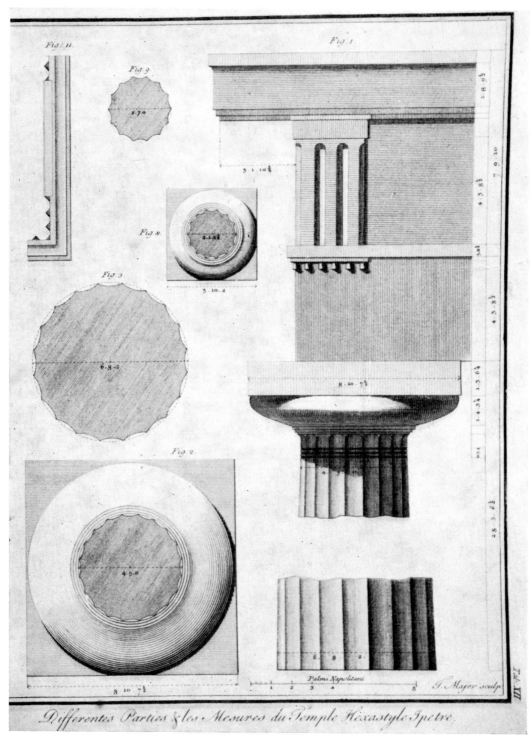

54. Doric Order (from Major, *Paestum*)

55. J. Bonomi. Church, Great Packington

56. J. Soane. Design for a Church

57. J. Soane. Project for a Mausoleum

58. Athens. Hephaesteion (from Stuart, *Antiquities*)

59. W. Wilkins. Grange Park

INDEX